To my dear Children
Randy and Debbie

It is a joy to work with you
in the developmental
this derivation

Don

"THOU WHO HATH BROUGHT US"

The Development of the
Seventh-day Adventist Denomination
Among African-Americans

Book One
Volume One

"…from the Cross to Emancipation"
31–1863
"Stony the road we've trod, bitter the chastening rod;
Born in the days when hope unborn had died.
Yet with a steady beat, did not our weary feet
Come to the place for which our fathers sighed."
—James Weldon Johnson

By
Charles E. Dudley, Sr., D. D., L. L. D.

Tamar Henley Corry, Editor

TEACH Services, Inc.
Brushton, New York

Copyright © 1997 Charles E. Dudley, Sr., D.D., L.L.D.

ISBN 1-57258-086-0
Library of Congress Catalog Card No. 97-60576

Published by

TEACH Services, Inc.
RR 1, Box 182
Brushton, New York 12916

Dedication

These volumes are dedicated to my mother, the late Julia Dudley, because of her love, devotion, protection and guidance and for instilling within us a trust in God when the road was long and during days of trial. She placed in us a determination to accept life for what it is and to share with others we met along the pathway.

...to my brothers and sisters, A. Gaynes, Alfred, Lucille and Martha, who through the years have been my pride and joy, my shelter and inspiration for higher achievements in life during my formative years.

...to my wife, Etta, who has walked beside me for fifty years down many rugged roads; through never ending storms and through good and trying times as we have our Christian experiences with those we love and sought to serve.

...to my children, Bonita, Charles, II, Albert, Sr. Benson, Edmund, Averil, Seth, Teresa and our grand children and to all of our family members who have brought an abundance of happiness, assurance and love.

We thank God for His guiding hand in our many endeavors.

Acknowledgments and Gratitude

My gratitude to Tamah Henley Curry for spending long hours editing these works and for placing them in evenly flowing perspective.

…to my son, Albert, consultant and promoter for the program.

…for the officers of the South Central Conference and Southern Union Conferences of Seventh-day Adventists for their encouragement and support in helping to lay the foundation for the project.

…for the senior citizens and others who helped to supply historical data and documents that have come to us through the years.

Expressions from Others Concerning the Author:

"Many of us are eagerly awaiting Charles Dudley's set of books on the origin and growth of the work of the Seventh-day Adventist Church in the African-American community. I have been privileged to have a sneak preview. What Doctor Dudley has put together is amazing. Like the griots of West Africa, Dudley is a walking history. He is also a tremendous researcher. Some of this findings will surprise you. But in every case you will be impressed with the way God has reached out to the sons and daughters of slaves and lifted them to unprecedented levels of corporate and personal growth and development. He has a story to tell!

Dr. C. E. Bradford, President Emeritus
of the North American Division
of the General Conference

"Dr. Charles E. Dudley has literally given his life to the Lord and to the Lord's work. He is a leader of many great accomplishments. His work is progress, unfailing productivity and consistent and graceful Christian witnessing. His un-sinkable confidence in God, his persistent optimism, his undying hope in and for our people have made him a beacon of light who inspires confidence and good will. He has borne bravely the slings and arrows of outrageous fortune, the ugly hostility of racism and, through it all, he has lit candles rather than curse the darkness His head is never bowed.

"These four volumes will bring light and inspiration to thousands who have been perpetually denied knowledge of their own history and accomplishments. They will also be a source of enlightenment to "fair-minded" men and women the world over who hunger for honesty, objectivity and truth. Dr. Dudley has carefully and painstakingly gathered his data from many sources and from the unimpeachable library of his own experience in an effective ministry which spans years of struggle, revolution and victory."

—Charles D. Brooks, former speaker for the
Breath of Life Telecast Ministries

"Charles Dudley is not only a historian, but he is a pioneer who has helped to make history. His insight and recollections deserve a place in the annals of SDA Black history."

—Delbert W. Baker, President, Oakwood College

"Charles Dudley has had a remarkable career as an administrator and spiritual leader in the Seventh day Adventist Church. He served as president of the South Central Conference for 31 years. That this is an elective office speaks to his confidence-inspiring leadership. He was leader of the Black Caucus for over 20 years and distinguished himself as a fearless advocate of

Black advancement. His impact in the treasures of financing, publishing, and negotiating change will outlive his time as many know. This document is the most comprehensive yet produced depicting the Black man's history in the Adventist church."

—*Earle E. Cleveland, "Evangelism Spark" for the World Church*
of Seventh-day Adventists; Lecturer, Dept. of Religion,
Oakwood College.

"Dr. Charles E. Dudley is an ordained minister of the Seventh-day Adventist Church and is presently pastoring two creditable churches in Tennessee. His educational achievements include specialized studies in techniques of modern management, organizational planning, thoughtful analysis of administrative effectiveness, and dynamics of successful leadership.

"He has held pastorates in Alabama, Louisiana, Mississippi, Texas, and Tennessee, but most of his active ministry has been in the field of administration as president of the South Central Conference for thirty-one years. He has served on numerous committees and has articles published in leading religious and professional journals. He is an effective preacher, administrator, lecturer, and writer and is courageously articulate in the championing of Black affairs.

"Beside the weighty responsibilities of ministry and administration and equally important responsibilities, he has been bless of God to provide church buildings and educational facilities to serve mankind. He has provided low-income housing for underprivileged and low-income families. He is sensitive to present day social, economic, political and educational conditions, particularly as they relate to African-Americans."

—*George R. Earle, President Emeritus - Northeastern Conference*

"This book is written by a personal, dear friend. He is a visionary leader who saw the church grow through many difficult years. It was a privilege to share his friendship as we worked together in the Southern Union."

—*Robert S., Folkenberg, President,*
General Conference of Seventh-day Adventists

"For more than twenty years, it has been my privilege to serve as a president and fellow administrator with Charles Dudley. He has been an inspiration to me through the years because of his deep commitment and dedication to service in the work our precious Saviour. His many years of consecrated service as well as his interest in Church History has made him an ideal person who has related to the progress of African-Americans from the cross to the present. All who read these volumes which cover the development of the work will be greater blessed, informed and inspired."

—*Malcholm D. Gordon, President,*
Southern Union Conference of Seventh-day Adventists

"C. E. Dudley's life extends across some of the most important and exciting years in the history of the Seventh-day Adventist Church.

"At this point in history, this generation needs to be made aware of the many events of the past which helped to bring to us the joys that we share today. The writer, a former administrator for more than four decades, feels morally obligated to reveal not only to Blacks, but to others, the milestones that have been attained by our people since the Seventh-day Adventist denomination first began accepting Blacks into the faith.

"This masterpiece is an eloquent expression concerning the lives of unsung pioneer heroes whom God used for the edifying of the body and to His glory in sharing the everlasting gospel with mankind. These volumes will aid people of all persuasions and in all walks of life to overcome the prevailing misguided concepts that may have developed within he hearts of many and to help them to better understand and appreciate the manner in which the Lord has used Black people to strengthen the work of the church. The body is stronger because of the successes that can be seen in the Black sector of the Seventh-day Adventist denomination."

—Lee A. Paschal, President Emeritus,
Oakwood College National Alumni Association;
Editor -North American Regional Voice
Journal and Retired Church Administrator

"It has been my privilege to know the author for several decades. His interest and commitment to the progress of African-American Adventists are legendary and without parallel. The reader will thrill with unceasing gratitude for the research documents and consistent intervention of Divine Providence.

"The church growth and conference planting among African-Americans legitimize the role and contributions of regional conferences. I recommend this unique treatment to 'Brown and Yellow, Black and White' as a permanent resource of historic value."

—Ralph P. Peay, President,
South Atlantic Conference and Chairman,
NAD Black Caucus of Seventh-day Adventists.

"The world church of Seventh-day Adventists in Black America - SDA, in particular, have benefited richly from the labors of Charles Edward Dudley. Paramount among his contributions is the situation of a sense of history so vital to self-worth and dignity.

"This present work, a valuable link to the past, demonstrates that fact and is a welcome addition to the enormous (Dudley File) of good works."

—Dr. Calvin B. Rock, Vice President,
World Church of Seventh-day Adventists

"THOU WHO HATH BROUGHT US"

The Development of the Seventh-day Adventist Denomination Among African-Americans

From the Cross to Emancipation
Book One - Volume One

Table of Contents

Introduction

One Sabbath afternoon while having dinner together, my grown children and some of their friends expressed to me their interest in knowing more about their religious, social, ethnic and biological roots. "Tell us about some of the things that happened back in your day!" they requested.

"Back in my day?" I questioned. "What do you mean?"

"We are interested in knowing more about our heritage and about the past events that have impacted the present. We want to know what circumstances brought us to where we are now!"

They were aware of my experience in Seventh-day Adventist denominational work, and knowing that I had done some research, they requested that I put in writing some of the historical data that I had gathered and/or experienced inside and outside of the Seventh-day Adventist Church through the years—events that helped to shape the present church.

Having served as a minister in the Seventh-day Adventist denomination for more than 49 years—18 as a church pastor and 31 as a conference administrator—I found it interesting that the officers of the Southern Union Conference, the Executive Committee of the South Central Conference and a number of my church leaders and members have made the same request over the years—that I share with them some of the events that helped to shape the church as it relates to Black people. What are some of the circumstances that helped to strengthen the work and to move us closer to the coming of the Lord and of the end of the age?

With these requests in mind, I am seeking to share with my dear friends, children, church members and others some of the blessings that the Lord has poured out on the African-American people and how He has used this people in many roles to help to advance the work of the gospel, not only in North America but around the world.

In recent years, there has been a plethora of literature—books, magazines, pamphlets—on the accomplishments of African-Americans before the days of slavery up to the present time. Regrettably, there is very little, if anything, written on the achievements of African-Americans with regard to the establishment, growth and development of the Seventh-day Adventist Church.

Like my cousin Alex Haley,[1] who in 1977 stimulated interest in searching for one's heritage and roots, I have always been fascinated by the study of the origin of things, people, religions, organizations, etc. Knowledge of family heritage or historical background contributes greatly to a person's sense of self-worth, dignity and self-esteem.

My elementary school teachers (Miss Mary Sullivan, Miss McCarten, Mr. L. L. Kemper, Mrs. Schyer, Miss Haggarty and Miss Bombrandy) in Indiana were from the old countries of Europe, and they instilled in us the concepts of religious freedom, patriotism, heritage, family pride and loyalty and a determination to complete any task that was begun. They brought to the classroom living experiences of their historical past in Europe and an appreciation for the struggles that their forefathers had endured to get to this "land of the free and home of the brave."

My parents Joseph and Julia Dudley, my Methodist Sunday School teachers Mrs. Goldie Carter and Mrs. Mary Weaver, the grown-ups in our neighborhood and my spiritual leaders (Pastor W. T. Beck, Mr. James Ulysus, Mr. James Higgins, Mr. Lonnie Luten, Mrs. Josephine Carter, Mrs. Lillian Luten) instilled within us a sense of dignity, self-worth, racial pride, steadfast trust in God and a love for mankind. They planted in our hearts a high regard for family, a concern for people and a sense of belonging. They taught us to care for each other and for all people, regardless of race, color, religion or national origin, community or station in life. Our neighborhood consisted of persons of all nationalities, kindred, ethnic groups and religious persuasions. We were family.

The old timers often related to us the challenges that their forefathers had endured under the oppression of slavery. They spoke, sang and preached about the blessings of the Almighty and how He helped them to "get over." Often in their praise they would be driven to tearful outbursts of thanksgiving and praise to God for their deliverance. Many were old enough to remember the days their parents and other relatives were held in slavery. In fact, my grandfather was 47 years old when the Emancipation Proclamation was signed; Grandma was just 19. I have listened to my uncles Nathan and Albert tell about the challenges they faced before they were set free. Four of my mother's brothers—Uncles Gentry, Nathan, John and Albert—experienced the ravages of

---

1   Alex Haley's aunt Mattie Palmer was married to my mother's first cousin Professor Charlie Fisher, the principal of the high school back in Hennin, Tennessee, many years ago. My grandfather Robert (Doc) Talley was born in Hennin, Tennessee, while his mother was a slave on the Talley plantation. Grandpa Talley's sister, Aunt Drucilla, married Robert (Bud) Fisher, the son of Frank Fisher of Hennin. Their son Charles married Mattie Palmer, whose niece was Bertha (Palmer) Haley, the mother of Alex, George and Julius Haley.

slavery. Some of them also spoke of seeing the stars fall from heaven in 1833. My Lord, what a morning when the stars began to fall!

The academic dean of one of the Seventh-day Adventist college boards on which I served once asked the question, "Why must there be a Negro History Week celebrated from year to year? Why not a Hispanic Week, Asian History Week or other ethnic history weeks? Why must there be a national holiday set aside in honor of Dr. Martin Luther King?" My response was, "It is because when the secular and religious history books were written, Blacks were not included unless they had done something bad, shameful or evil."

Lerone Bennett, the Black historian for Ebony Magazine states: "Long before Black Americans made headlines on the playing field, they were making history and lots of it in fields like medicine, exploration, industry and on the field of battle. The names of these early 'all stars' probably are not on the tip of one's tongue because they were not in most history books until recent years after insistence that Blacks had made lasting contributions to the development and growth of the church, the nation and the world."

Among the names that come to my mind are: Dr. Daniel Hale Williams, Matthew Henson, Benjamin Banneker, Chrispus Attucks, Dr. Charles Drew, Dr. George Washington Carver, Booker T. Washington, W. E. B. Dubois, Harriet Tubman, Sojourner Truth, Frederick Douglass, William Foye, Thurgood Marshall, James Weldon Johnson, Thomas H. Allison, Hanna More, Thomas Branch, Charles M. Kinney, Joseph H. Laurence, J. Gershom Dasent, Attorney W. H. Green, Mrs. Christine Thompson, Dr. Natelkka Burrell, Dr. Frank W. Hale, Jr., Dr. J. Mark Cox, Dr. T. M. R. S. Howard, Dr. Martin Luther King, Jr., Dr. Eva B. Dykes, Dr. Carl Ashley Dent, Dr. E. Earle Cleveland, Eric C. Ward, Dr. Charles E. Bradford, General Colin Powell, Frank L. Peterson, G. E. Peters, Colonel Leonard Johnson, Elder Benjamin W. Abney, Sr., Elder Calvin E. Moseley, Jr., Dr. Harry Ford. And the list is endless.

There are thousands of these unsung heroes—enough to fill a library. Thanks to the efforts of these Blacks and many others, the Black history weeks and months from year to year help to remind us just how far we have come by the grace of God.

African-Americans rise to their feet whenever the Negro national anthem is heard or sung. "Lift every voice and sing 'till earth and heaven ring, ring with the harmony of liberty (freedom)." This was the rallying call of James Weldon Johnson, its author, when he set the words to music. Our forefathers had come through storms, struggles, hardship, heartaches, trials, dangers and snares to achieve their long-sought-for freedom. With the song, Johnson indelibly stamped into the hearts of the people the fact that it was God who had brought them along the stormy roads to their long-hoped-for freedom.

In these volumes, we will seek to tell the story of this long struggle from the cross on which Jesus died to the emancipation joys, to the struggle for survival in an unfriendly world, to the dawn of a new day of progress and achievement, to today's determination to keep moving ahead until the goal is reached. To this end, we will share with our young friends and older ones alike, with friends of all races and nationalities some of the history of the Seventh-day Adventist denomination as it relates to the contributions that Black people have made to the growth and development of the church. There are many names that do not appear, but we just cannot tell it all. I trust that it will be revealing and enlightening.

The roots of the Seventh-day Adventist denomination can be traced back to the continent of Africa; however, historians have led many to believe that the Christian religion had its origin in Europe before the discovery of America and the New World. Long before America as a nation existed, Africans were following and sharing the tenets of Christianity. The Seventh-day Adventist denomination often refers to itself as the "remnant" of the Christian church that Jesus left on earth when He returned to His Father in heaven, with this remnant having all of the basic characteristics and teachings of the original Christian church.

This first volume covers the period of time from the cross in A.D. 31 to the emancipation in 1863 when African slaves in America were set free. During this period, slavery became a lucrative industry, the United States of America as a nation began to leave its imprint on the pages of history, a miscalculation by some Christians that the time had come for the Lord to return to earth brought terrible disappointment to the Christian world, the Seventh-day Adventist denomination was officially organized and took its place among the religions of the world, a colored lady was appointed by God to give guidance to the Seventh-day Adventist Church, African slaves were liberated and forces set in motion to prepare them to be a part of the heavenly host when the kingdom finally comes.

The second volume covers the period from 1863 to 1900. These were challenging years when the races had to adjust to their new social status. This adjustment on the part of Blacks meant "climbing up the rough side of the mountain." Changes in lifestyles brought trauma to the hearts of both races. It was a time of social, political, economic and religious struggles and challenges. Many Whites looked upon Blacks as being three-fifths human with no soul to save. They were considered as beasts of the field or as property to be bought and sold as the master saw fit. However, the Lord continued to watch over our forefathers, to impress upon their hearts a sense of determination and self-worth, and to endow them with the ability to fend for themselves.

Many in the Seventh-day Adventist Church were reluctant to accept these people into membership in their congregations. During the days of slavery, Blacks had attended the worship services with their masters. Now they began to establish houses of worship of their own.

Often, the names of Edson White, E. B. Lane, Silas Osborne and Dr. J. C. Caldwell, among others, are credited with pioneering the "work" of sharing Adventism with Blacks in the South, but history reveals that before these brave souls ventured South, Black leaders had already begun to establish pockets of Seventh-day Adventist believers in a number of places. Under the teachings of Harry Lowe, Alonzo Barry, Alonzo Parker, Thomas Allison and other members of the race, believers were already following the biblical principles of the church and inviting others to join them.

At the turn of the century when Black leaders began teaching and preaching the gospel to their own people, this sector of the denomination was blessed with rapid growth in membership and new congregations. This growth was not without problems from the church leaders; however, the Lord continued to bless the work among these people in North America. Further development finally led to the establishment of separate administrative units, called Regional Conferences, in 1945 to supervise the work among this people. This progress took the church by surprise. This period reflects how the Lord "brought us thus far on our way."

The final period begins in 1945 and extends to the present, during which time Blacks continued directing their own destinies and working for their own people. Evangelistic efforts mushroomed, the work force grew, new congregations and schools were established and the influence of Black growth and development extended to other nations of the world. Many began to catch the vision of a completed work and the imminent establishment of the kingdom of heaven, and they joined forces to "keep on climbing until we reach our heavenly goal."

The purpose of these volumes is to share the events and challenges through which African-Americans have come in seeking to be prepared to meet the Lord when He comes again. The story will not end until the kingdom of heaven comes and the church on earth unites with the church in glory. May it be soon!

"I have endeavored to select and group together events in the history of the church in such a manner as to trace the unfolding of the great testing truths that at different periods have been given to the world, that have excited the wrath of Satan, and the enmity of a world-loving church, and that have been maintained by the witness of those who 'loved not their lives unto the death.' " (Rev. 12:11.)—*The Great Controversy*, p. xi

Charles E. Dudley, Sr.
President Emeritus of the
South Central Conference
of Seventh-day Adventists

Foreword

JUBILEE

Ezra Watts

Ezra was his name. Ezra Watts. He arrived at Oakwood Junior College during the 1930s from Soso, Mississippi. Many Black Seventh-day Adventists have their roots in Soso. Among them are the Knights whose heroine was Anna, the first colored missionary to serve the church in India; she served there for 16 years. There were also the Booths, the Crosbys, the Crossgroves, and the Watts. The Greens, the Moffetts, the Henris, the Doves, and the Woodfoxes came later. They were all related, so to speak.

Anna had learned of the Seventh-day Adventist denomination by reading tracts sent to her by Miss Edith I. Embree of Oakland, California, and W. W. Eastman of Texas. She joined the church and later taught her entire community what she had learned from her study of the Bible. Others joined the faith, including Miss Gracie her sister, Sidney her brother and his wife Mrs. Allie. Many of her nieces and nephews also accepted this new-found faith, including Homer, Horace, Hollis, Hannan, Roscoe, Tazwell, Hester and Henrietta, along with their cousins Ezra, VanBuren and Curtis Watts from nearby Sumrall.

Anna Knight

Many of them attended Oakwood Junior College in Huntsville, Alabama. In fact, so many of them were enrolled there at one time that there was a saying among the students that the song should never be sung at Oakwood "there is no 'Knight' there!"

Members of the Soso, Mississippi Church

Ezra was tall, lean and strong as a bull and was attending Oakwood to study education and prepare himself to be a teacher. He made a strong impact with songs he had learned from the folks back home on the farm. One that became a favorite

15

of the students was called "Jubilee." The quartet of Fred Crowe, Walter Kissack, James Christopher and Joseph Wilkins included it in their repertoire and often sang it while on tour.

"Jubilee" meant a day of freedom. Leviticus 25:10 states, "And ye shall hallow the fiftieth year, and proclaim liberty throughout all the land unto all the inhabitants thereof: it shall be a jubilee unto you; and ye shall return every man unto his possession, and ye shall return every man unto his family."

In biblical days when an Israelite was held in bondage by his brother, every seven-year period was declared a time of release. No one could be sold into bondage; all debts were forgiven; no payment for debts could be collected. A person holding a mortgage or a debt had to forfeit his claim at the end of the seven-year period. This was done for seven seven-year periods. After the forty-ninth year and during the fiftieth year, everyone everywhere was set free. It was a year of "at-one-ment." It was a special year of jubilee. No one could be held as a captive or be enslaved during the fiftieth year.

While this was the practice in biblical times, no such jubilee was envisioned for Africans who were brought to the New World in slavery. From the perspective of slave masters, the institution of slavery was to be forever; however, some slaves who learned to read the Bible found the passage about the year of jubilee and with anticipation sang, "There's going to be a jubilee down in the old campground." They sang of freedom. They prayed for freedom. They hoped for freedom. They planned for freedom. They fought and died to be free. They looked forward to the day when all of God's children would be free.

The words of Ezra's song, "There's going to be a jubilee way down in the old campground," had a special meaning for many African-Americans. The time of jubilee was long anticipated by the slaves. Each generation hoped that one day freedom would come. During the years from 1444 to 1863, African-Americans experienced a long march from slavery to freedom. Many laid down their lives with a steadfast hope for that day and a determination to make it a reality. Many endured privation, affliction, agony and shame so that their descendants might experience the freedoms that they themselves could not enjoy.

16

Nowhere are there more monuments to the jubilee theme held by the slaves than at Fisk University in Nashville, Tennessee. There is a music hall named Jubilee Hall and a bridge, called the Fisk Jubilee Singers Memorial Bridge, leading to the school. While going through financial straits during its beginning years, school officials sent the Fisk Jubilee Singers,[2] who had performed for the royalties of Europe and the aristocrats of American society, to raise funds to help keep the school's doors open.

As we review events that took place from the beginning of slavery to its end, we also will focus on the enslavement into which mankind fell when Adam and Eve sinned six thousand years ago and on Jesus Christ, the Son of God, who left His Father's side in heaven to bring freedom to all.

Jesus commissioned His followers to tell the good news of freedom to the entire human race. Unfortunately, for centuries men began to enslave each other instead of carrying out the mission of freedom. Africans seemed to have suffered most severely when they were enslaved in America for four hundred years. And the kingdom for which the Christians prayed could not become a reality until all people were free.

This book traces events from the death of Jesus Christ on the cross of Calvary in 31 A.D. up to 1863, when African-Americans were liberated, and onward to the time when ultimate freedom will be realized at the second coming of Christ and the end of this present world. According to Martin Luther King, Jr., "We know through painful experience that freedom is never voluntarily given by the oppressor; it must be demanded by the oppressed."—*Why We Can't Wait*, by Martin Luther King, Jr., p. 80

Adherents to the Seventh-day Adventist denomination consider themselves the "remnant" of the original church Jesus left when He returned to heaven. From its inception, African-Americans have struggled to be considered a part of this remnant. Despite some resistance, they have witnessed the love and mercies of God as they sought to prepare for Jesus' triumphal return to earth for every nation, kindred, tongue and people. That event will mark the eternal day of jubilee for all His people—red, yellow, Black and White. And when we "all" get to heaven, what a day!

I trust that you will enjoy reading the story that has brought us this far, by faith.

---

2   Two of the original singers were members of the Seventh-day Adventist Church. The Fisk Jubilee Singers made the Negro spiritual acceptable in society and the music world. Before the group began touring, Negro spirituals were regarded as "plantation songs" sung only by the slaves and without meaning in the cultural circles of the day.

Chapter 1

The Gospel For All Of Mankind

"And I saw another angel fly in the midst of heaven, having the everlasting gospel to preach unto them that dwell on the earth, and to every nation, and kindred, and tongue, and people." Revelation 14:6

The long-awaited day was finally here! The air was filled with expectancy. A sense of anticipated relief from the burdens of this life, mingled with the glorious expectation of an imminent meeting with their Lord, filled the hearts of the group of Advent believers gathered on October 22, 1844, to await the return of Jesus to earth.

There were Episcopalians, Methodists, and Baptists, with at least one thing in common. They had accepted the teachings of William Miller, whose study of the 2300-day prophecy of Daniel 2, 7, 8, 9 and 10 had led him to conclude that Jesus would return for His followers on that date.

Most, if not all, of the farmers in the group had left their crops.[3] in the fields. The believers had ceased all secular activities and were waiting for Jesus to come. But when October 22 ended and Jesus had not come, a bitter disappointment engulfed them. Where had they gone wrong?

Interest in Jesus' coming had been building since 1833, when meteoric showers sparkled the heavens. Everything the Advent believers had studied pointed to that date as the beginning of the judgment, which, as they understood it, meant the end of the world.

One by one, disappointed members of the group had to reexamine their beliefs. Some held firm to the belief that Jesus would come, but they conceded that the calculation of the specific date was wrong. After further study, it became clear to many that October 22, 1844, signaled the beginning of the

---

3   Leaving the crops in the ground would later be a blessing because harvested crops were destroyed by potato rot, which struck the country in 1844. J. N. Loughborough in his book *Rise and Progress of the Seventh-day Adventist Church*, p. 86. 86, states: "As the fall was mild, and Brother Hastings' potatoes were left in the ground until November, none of them rotted. Consequently, he had an abundant supply for himself and his unfortunate neighbors who had been so solicitous for his welfare the previous October, and who, in the spring, were obliged to buy seed potatoes of him, and were glad to get them by paying a good price. What they had supposed was going to be such a calamity to Brother Hastings, God turned to a temporal blessing, not only to him, but to his neighbors also."

"...to every nation, kindred, tongue and people."

investigative judgment in the heavenly courts to determine who, among those professing to be Christ's followers, would be ready to meet Him at His coming. It meant that instead of coming to earth, Christ was entering another phase of His priestly ministry on behalf of fallen man and was moving from the holy place to the most holy place of the heavenly sanctuary.

Christ could not return to earth in 1844. He Himself had given the commission in Mark 16:15, "Go ye into all the world, and preach the gospel...." And in Matthew 24:14, He said, "And this gospel of the kingdom shall be preached in all the world...and then shall the end come." In Revelation 14:6, John recorded seeing another angel flying in the midst of heaven with the everlasting gospel to preach unto "every nation, and kindred, and tongue, and people."

The Bible clearly indicates that the carrying out of the commission to preach the gospel was to precede Christ's coming. One of the reasons the glorious event did not take place in 1844 was that the gospel of God's love and of His saving grace had not yet been preached in India or to the nations of Asia, Africa and the Americas. And, notably, the Black people in the Western Hemisphere were still in slavery.

But what does slavery have to do with Christ's second coming? The year before the bitter disappointment, Henry Highland Garnett, a Methodist preacher, had urged slaves attending the Methodist Convention in Buffalo, New York, to seek freedom because the Lord would not save them as long as they were in slavery. Vincent Harding tells of Garnett's speech to the slaves as follows:

"In his address to the slaves, Garnett told the southern bondmen that they must resist slavery because the White-controlled system of bondage made it impossible for them to obey the biblical command 'to keep the Sabbath day holy...to search the Scriptures...and bring up your children with respect for God's laws, and to worship no other God but Him.' Therefore his central, motivating call was a strange one, placing an almost bizarre burden upon the Black children of bondage: they must seek freedom from slavery, because only as free men and women could they keep God's laws and reap the heavenly reward. Garnett warned the enslaved masses, 'You are not certain of heaven, because you suffer yourselves to remain in a state of slavery, where you cannot obey the commandments of the Sovereign of the universe.' "—*There is a River*, pp. 141, 142.

Ellen G. White, a well-known and respected leader and author of the Seventh-day Adventist Church, had a similar view about the plight of the slaves. In her book *Early Writings*, she states:

"I saw the slave master will have to answer for the soul of his slave whom he has kept in ignorance; and the sins of the slave will be visited upon the master. God cannot take to heaven the slave who has been kept in ignorance

21

and degradation, knowing nothing of God or the Bible, fearing nothing but his master's lash, and holding a lower position than the brutes. But He does the best thing for him (the slave) that a compassionate God can do. He permits him to be as if he had not been, while the master must endure the seven last plagues and then come up in the second resurrection and suffer the second, most awful death. Then the justice of God will be satisfied."—*Early Writings*, p. 276.

The question of a little gray-haired Bible instructor, Ella Johnson, I met as a young preacher in 1947 is relevant here. She asked, "How are Black people in the United States represented in Revelation 14:6?" The text says, "And I saw another angel fly in the midst of heaven having the everlasting gospel to preach unto them that dwell on the earth, and to every nation, and kindred, and tongue, and people." Answering her own question, she mused, "We are not a nation, nor a kindred. We do not have a tongue (language). We are just 'people.' All mixed up people."

Although African-Americans have roots in Africa and the African slave trade, they are not Africans. They are Americans whose blood has been mixed with that of people from every nation, kindred, tongue and people on planet earth.

This group of people was not adequately represented among the Adventists who looked for Christ's coming in 1844. There were a few Blacks among the Adventists in 1844, but a large number still suffered under the system of slavery. And because of this and other reasons stated, Jesus could not come. To use a legal scenario, when the Judge of all the earth looked over the courtroom, He issued a "summary judgment," instead of a direct verdict, because all nations, kindred, tongue and people were not represented. As slaves, the vast number of Blacks were not free to hear or accept the gospel (they were denied the opportunity to read, therefore, were not responsible for their sinful deeds and would not be called to account for them in the investigative judgment of Daniel 5).

At its origin before the foundations of the world were laid, the gospel of Jesus Christ did not exclude the Black people who had been transplanted to the United States of America. They were included in the plan of salvation from the beginning, along with peoples of all nations, kindred and tongue. And they were to be saved, not as slaves but as free people, able to make choices about their salvation.

When Jesus began His early ministry, He announced: "The Spirit of the Lord is upon me, because he hath anointed me (1) to preach the gospel (good news of deliverance from sin) to the poor; he hath sent me (2) to heal the broken hearted, (3) to preach deliverance to the captives and (4) recovering of sight to the blind, (5) to set at liberty (give freedom to) them that are bruised, and (6) to preach the acceptable year of the Lord." Luke 4:18, 19.

"These...elements outline Jesus' mission as the Messiah.... Some commentators see these elements as having primarily a spiritual application. In this sense, good news to the poor would mean to the poor in spirit, people who need salvation. The captives and prisoners would be those bound by sin, who need release from the grip of Satan. Others see these verses as a call for social justice for those who are literally poor, blind, and in prison (enslaved)."

"When we think of the poor, we usually think in terms of financial poverty, but it is not only lack of money or material resources that makes people outcasts. In Jewish society, anyone with a major disease was an outcast because it was commonly believed that all disease was a punishment by God for personal or inherited sin. Thus, a blind person was an outcast of society, but to Jesus, he or she was one of the 'poor' whom He came to save. Tax collectors like Matthew were among the wealthiest people in the community, but, by Jewish standards, they were outcasts, unworthy of salvation because of their collaboration with the Roman government. Samaritans (people of color) were not even considered part of the human race. They were certainly 'prisoners' in terms of social fellowship...Jesus' treatment of people from all classes of society, His never failing love, sympathy, and concern for the outcast and the oppressed, was one of the strongest evidences of His Messiahship. Paul would later remark, 'The saying is sure and worthy of full acceptance, that Christ Jesus came into the world to save sinners' (1 Tim. 1:15, NRSV)."—
Adult Sabbath School Lessons, Teachers Edition, Oct., Nov., Dec. 1995, p. 69.

If the gospel story had been shared with all people, it would have brought true and everlasting freedom to those who had been in slavery for centuries. It would have freed the mind, the body and the soul. It would have lifted ignorance and superstition from the eyes of oppressed souls. This work had to be done before there could be any heavenly home going.

So, while the Advent believers were joyful at the prospect of leaving the cares of this world behind in 1844, their work was unfinished. "You must prophesy again!" came the injunction from Revelation 10:11. God desires that all of His children would be ready to meet Jesus when He returns. The slaves were not ready in 1844. They were not presented with the opportunity to get ready. The Advent believers thought that they would leave the slaves behind, but this was not God's plan. "God having provided some better thing for us, that they without us should not be made perfect." Hebrews 11:40. More teaching, preaching, reaching and sharing of the gospel had to be done. God had a plan for this people that must be carried out. "And this gospel of the kingdom shall be preached in all the world...and then shall the end come." Matthew 24:14.

Chapter 2

Africa, Oh Africa

"Princes shall come out of Egypt; Ethiopia shall soon stretch out her hands unto God." Psalms 68:31

Elephant

Persons who claim Africa as the Motherland should be encouraged by the fact that Black people are, and have always been, recipients of God's special favor, and that they enjoy a heritage rich with God's blessings. Vestiges of these blessings on the African continent are evident in the many precious and rich natural resources such as gold, silver, copper, diamonds and oil that remain on the land until this day.

Africa, peacefully surrounded by the Atlantic and Indian Oceans and the Mediterranean Sea, is the land of many firsts. Civilization originated there. Craftsmanship of all kinds had its beginning in African ingenuity. Cultures and organizations of governments began in Africa. But even more significant than all of these is the fact that it was on this continent, the largest one on the globe, that the Lord planted the Garden of Eden at the beginning of earth's history. He created our first parents, Adam and Eve, from its soil.

Hutu Tribe—Rwanda

Etta Dudley visiting Rwanda family

Giraffe

Charles E. Dudley visits with Watusi Chief

The country of Egypt produced food for Jacob's family during the seven years of famine recorded in Genesis 42. Although born of Jewish lineage, Jesus was carried to the same African country of Egypt centuries later, and it served as a haven to shelter and protect Him from the fierce anger of King Herod, who had sought to kill all the baby boys rather than to acknowledge the birth of the Messiah, the future king of all the earth.

In the beginning there was one speech, one blood and one people. When man disobeyed God, the garden was taken to heaven; however, many rich natural resources remained on the continent. God endowed man whom He had made in His image and after His likeness with the ability to think, to plan and to develop this earth to His glory. However, when sin entered into the world, the minds of men began to degenerate, leading to evil and wickedness of all description. Death and decay began to plague mankind, nature, animals and the elements throughout this vast universe. God was compelled to destroy the wickedness with a flood.

Shortly after the flood, during which God saved Noah and his family in the ark, the distinctions among nations, kindred, tongues and people began to emerge. Reasoning that they had to do something to preserve the human race in the event of another flood, the descendants of Noah began to construct a tower that they hoped would be high enough to provide them security. But God was displeased. These plans were not in harmony with His will. And He confounded the language, so that construction of the Tower of Babel had to be halted. The plan had originated with Ham's descendant Nimrod, who became the first architect and builder on the earth. He was a Black man.

As the descendants of Noah's sons—Shem, Ham and Japheth—sought to recover from this apparent setback, they began to migrate from their African homeland to other parts of the earth. They separated based on their differences and congregated to form linguistic clusters based on their similarities. The children of Shem settled in the milder climatic regions of the Middle East; the sons of Ham chose to remain near the African continent; and Japheth's offspring chose Europe. In time, each settlement developed its own culture and ethnicity. Each served God in its own way, if at all; but many were aware of the "Great Spirit" through whom they lived, moved and existed.

Biblical history centers mostly around the children of Shem in the Middle East and the children of Ham in Africa. The pages of Holy Writ cast many of these people of African ancestry in various roles as they wandered unto and off the stage of biblical history. Hagar, Sarah's handmaid, was an Egyptian woman. When Sarah and Abraham decided to use her to help God fulfill His own promise to Abraham, this African woman gave birth to Ishmael, the father of the Arab nations of the Middle East (Genesis 16). This led to family disputes between the two wives (nations of people); but Abraham blessed both groups. Elder J. H. Laurence, a former evangelist of the Seventh-day Adventist Church interprets these blessings to be in the form of "things on top of the earth for the children of Isaac and those things below the earth (oil, etc.) to the children of Ishmael." Today's trouble in the Middle East is between the descendants of both sons, not so much over territory as over what is in the earth under the territory (oil).

Moses, the great leader who led Israel from Egyptian bondage, took Zipporah, an Ethiopian (African) woman, as his wife (Numbers 12:1). Caleb, the Kenezite (of African descent), was a faithful and courageous man who held to the promises of God when the children of Israel finally reached the land of promise (Joshua 14:6). Simeon, called Niger, was authorized by God to ordain Paul for his special ministry (Acts 13:1, 2).

Perhaps one of the most significant contributions by an African to the pages of the Scriptures was that of one Simon, a Cyrenian African, who relieved the physically exhausted Saviour of the burden of the heavy wooden cross and carried it to Calvary. Ellen G. White's account of Simon's contribution in her book, *Desire of Ages* states:

"The crowd that followed the Saviour saw His weak and staggering steps, but they manifested no compassion…. None even of the mob that followed Him would stoop to bear the cross.

"At this time a stranger, Simon a Cyrenian, coming in from the country, meets the throng. He hears the taunts and ribaldry of the crowd; he hears the words contemptuously repeated, Make way for the King of the Jews! He stops in astonishment at the scene; and as he expresses his compassion, they seize him and place the cross upon his shoulders.

"Simon had heard of Jesus. His sons were believers in the Saviour but himself was not a disciple. The bearing of the cross to Calvary was a blessing to Simon, and he was ever after grateful for this providence. It led him to take upon himself the cross of Christ from choice, and ever cheerfully stand beneath its burden."—*Desire of Ages*, p. 742.

Another African, whose brief but highly significant appearance on the stage of action must be noted, is the Ethiopian eunuch. This man was instructed by Philip and went on his way rejoicing with the gospel truths back to his homeland (Acts 8:29–39). Evidence that he must have been convincing in spreading the gospel story is supported by the fact that Christianity was well established in Ethiopia during the fifth and sixth centuries, and Ethiopian rulers were strong defenders of Christianity. It is reported that in A.D. 523, an Ethiopian king led an expedition into southern Arabia to punish those responsible for the massacre of Christians. In *The History of Black Catholics in the United States*, Cyrian Davis states that Ethiopia was known as a Christian nation with its own tradition and culture. He further asserts that "in the history of the church, Ethiopia occupies a special place. Here we have an African church that has its roots in the early church. Before the church was established in Ireland or Anglo-Saxon England or in any country of northern Europe, a

Catholic church linked to St. Atnansius blossomed in an African culture. Despite any doctrinal differences that arose later, the Ethiopian church is a reminder that Africa forms part of the rich heritage of Catholicism."—*The History of Black Catholics in the United States*, p. 8.

The Scripture's reassurance that Ethiopia (Africa) would again stretch forth her hand to serve God offers continued affirmation of the special role this great continent and its people have been called upon by God to fulfill.

There is evidence that many tenets of Christianity were preserved through African people down through the centuries. When the division of the races took place, different groups migrated to various parts of the world; however, the basic teachings concerning God as Creator, Sustainer and coming King were held. During the successive rulership of the Babylonians, the Medo-Persians and the Greeks and when Rome first ascended to power, history reveals that Christian beliefs were strongly upheld on the continent of Africa. It was not until Rome ascended to power that the rights of this blessed people to practice their religious convictions were challenged.

Historians' depiction of Africa as the "dark continent" and of its people as "heathens" is erroneous. Ellen G. White writes: "Amid the gloom of the Dark Ages, the Christians of Central Africa were lost sight of and forgotten by the world, and for many centuries they enjoyed freedom in the exercise of their faith."—*The Great Controversy*, p. 577.

The story is told that a French statesman gave an African slave to his son, who took the slave to be his personal friend. They spent their childhood, adolescence, and early adult years together. The son even carried the slave to school with him when he went to Prussia for studies. They studied side by side and excelled to the point that they both received their doctorate degrees together. The African Anton Wilhelm Amo became one of the most sought after instructors on the university level; however he returned to Africa and was never heard from since.

Addi Okum—Nigeria and
Benson Mugemancuro—Rwanda

Chapter 3

Preservers Of The Sabbath

Africans and African-Americans are not generally thought of as being observers of the seventh-day Sabbath. One Sunday morning while on a flight from Jackson, Mississippi, to Memphis, Tennessee, it was my pleasure to have Dr. Benjamin E. Hooks, the former executive secretary of the N.A.A.C.P. as my seat mate. Our paths had crossed on many previous occasions when we both served as ministers in Memphis during the 1950s. In the course of our conversation, he expressed surprise to learn that many Black people in the United States and around the world are members of the Seventh-day Adventist Church.

It is not surprising that some people are unaware that many African-Americans are members of the Seventh-day Adventist Church. African-Americans have traditionally been members of the Methodist and Baptist churches. Many members of other denominations have never even heard of the Seventh-day Adventist Church; others are only aware that its members observe Saturday as the day of worship as do orthodox Jews. Very few people are aware of the contributions that Seventh-day Adventists have made to the religious world.

One little known fact is that African people observed the Sabbath in the same tradition as Jesus did while He was on earth. The remnant of the original Christian church established by Jesus before He returned to heaven remained on the African continent and held to all the basic teachings of the Scriptures, including Sabbathkeeping. In recognition of the Lord as Creator, this remnant continued to keep the biblical, seventh-day Sabbath and preserved Sabbathkeeping through the ages.

African Sabbath keepers were among those captured and carried to Europe, and they carried their Christian beliefs and practices, including Sabbathkeeping, with them. Most European captors were loathed to accept the religion of the captives, but few did, thus preserving the Sabbath among Africans and Europeans.

As Rome, the fourth and final world ruler, assumed power, papal and pagan forces formed alliances with each other, which led to compromises in Christian beliefs. Unfortunately, not all Africans were preservers of the truth. According to *The History of Black Catholics in the United States*, by Cyrian Davis, three popes of African descent served the Catholic Church during this period and were instrumental in forging alliances that led to changes in the beliefs and practices of the Christian church. They were St. Victor I (ca.186–

ca.197), St. Miltiades (311–314), and St. Gelasius (492–496). *The Oxford Dictionary of Popes* by J. N. D. Kelly details the contribution of these popes to the popular worship practices of their time. Pope Gelasius, probably the most influential of the three, declared the "infallibility" of the pope, instituted the "primacy of the Holy See," introduced pomp and circumstance to the church, and set before the people collections of prayers and texts for the mass.

Under the African popes, compromises were entered into with heathen rulers. Emperor Constantine became a member of the Christian faith and by 321 A.D. was instrumental in forging a coalition between the church and the government. The state carried out the wishes of the church with political enforcement. Sunday was substituted for Saturday as the day of worship. Easter was established as the first Sunday after the vernal equinox and was tied to sun worship by a people who believed that the sun controlled the seasons, the growth and development of crops and various aspects of man's existence. These people had knowledge of the true and living God, who blotted out the sun when Israel was in Egypt (Exodus 10:21–23), who commanded the sun to stand still at Jericho (Joshua 10:12) and who ordered it to back up when Hezekiah became ill (1 Kings 20:11). They were aware that the sun refused to shine when Jesus Christ died on the Roman cross at Calvary (Luke 23:44). The heathen leaders knew the power of the true and living God but refused to worship him. Nevertheless, Christian leaders made compromises with this people by establishing Sunday worship. When the African pope suggested a change in the day of worship, there was division among the African people. While most of the then-known world observed the change in the day of worship, some Africans held to the true Sabbath. "Womcombo," an African term meaning "No work today," was used to vocalize the position of Africans who chose the true Sabbath over the man-made day of worship.

Other compromises led to December 25 being set aside as the date to celebrate the "Christ mass" (Christmas). Heathen images were introduced into Christian worship. Latin was adopted as the language for worship purposes. The Vatican, the seven steeples or hills in Rome, became the permanent location for the Holy See.

The Roman government and Roman church made inquisitions of Christians who refused to yield their convictions and principles as set forth by Christ. Many of these people suffered persecution; many surrendered their lives rather than choosing to disobey God. They held firm to their faith. Ellen G. White recorded:

"A striking illustration of Rome's policy toward those who disagree with her was given in the long and bloody persecution of the Waldenses, some of whom were observers of the Sabbath. Others suffered in a similar manner for their fidelity to the fourth commandment. The history of the churches of Ethiopia and Abyssinia is especially significant.... An edict was issued forbidding the observance of the Sabbath under the severest penalties. But papal tyranny soon became a yoke so galling that the Abyssinians determined to break it from their necks. After a terrible struggle the Romanists were banished from their dominions, and the ancient faith was restored....

"The churches of Africa held the Sabbath as it was held by the papal church before her complete apostasy. While they kept the seventh day in obedience to the commandment of God, they abstained from labor on the Sunday in conformity to the custom of the church. Upon obtaining supreme power, Rome had trampled upon the Sabbath of God to exalt her own; but the churches of Africa, hidden for nearly a thousand years, did not share in this apostasy. When brought under the sway of Rome, they were forced to set aside the true and exalt the false Sabbath; but no sooner had they regained their independence than they returned to obedience to the fourth commandment."— *The Great Controversy*, pp. 577, 578.

When the entire European Christian world accepted Sunday as a day of worship, Blacks in Ethiopia still kept the seventh-day Sabbath, in accordance with the teachings of the Bible.

The day of worship acknowledges God as the Creator of the universe. "Thus the heavens and the earth were finished, and all the host of them. And on the seventh day God ended his work which he had made; and he rested on the seventh day from all his work which he had made. And God blessed the seventh day, and sanctified it: because that in it he had rested from all his work which God created and made." Genesis 2:1–3.

As observers of the true Sabbath, Africans acknowledged God not only as Creator but as Sustainer, Redeemer and coming King. Black people have been keeping the Sabbath since the days Jesus was on the earth to show their regard and respect for Him and His word. Ethiopians were keeping the Sabbath when the slave trade began in 1441, and they were still keeping the Sabbath in 1935 when Benito Mussolini of Italy declared war at the beginning of World War II. The Seventh-day Adventist influence was strongly felt in the country under the leadership of Haile Selassie, the descendant of David. In 1994 there were 97,930 Seventh-day Adventist Sabbath-keeping Ethiopians in Ethiopia, not to speak of hundreds of the Coptic Church who still observe the seventh-day Sabbath in recognition of the Lord as God alone.

The following quotation from Russell Thomsen's book *Seventh-day Baptists* is pertinent here:

"England is many things to many people...to the Seventh-day Baptists and Seventh-day Adventists England means more...for it was there among people of strong religious conviction and deep piety, incessant in their search for truth and freedom, that pre-Reformation ancestors of seventh-day Sabbath keepers lived, preached and died...Historical intimations suggest an unbroken line of Sabbath keepers in Britain from the time Christianity was first intro-

CHURCH LEADERS IN AFRICA

Visiting with the Mwsai Tribe in Kenya

A Sabbath keeper in Zambia

One hundred-four year old African SDA pastor who introduced the missionaries to the Solusi tribe in Rhodesia

duced there…. Of interest to Irish history is the probability that St. Patrick was a seventh-day Sabbath keeper.

"The Waldenses…were purists…some among them no doubt clung to the true Sabbath, even at the threat of life. For about three centuries some church historians believe, they kept the light of the seventh-day Sabbath burning in England. Their distinct witness came to an end in the British Isles around 1315, when the group was generally merged with the Lollards, many of whom also observed the Sabbath of Jehovah."—Seventh-day Baptists, pp. 9–12, 14, 24.

When Bishop Charles H. Mason founded the Church of God in Christ (Pentecostal) in 1907, little did he realize that some of its members would adhere to keeping the seventh-day Sabbath in their worship to the true and living God.

The Sabbath has been preserved by the African people through the centuries since the cross, and others today observe this day as the true day of worship. Others who keep the Sabbath are the Baptists, some members of the Holiness churches and many in Europe and other parts of the world. There are millions of colored people around the world who are remembering the Sabbath day and keeping it holy. It is a blessing that the Lord inspired people on the continent of Africa to preserve Sabbathkeeping. Saturday, the seventh day of the week, remains in the same weekly cycle as it has been from creation when God blessed and hallowed it. He commanded mankind to recognize it as the day that acknowledges Him as the Creator, Sustainer and Ruler over all things throughout the universe. Saturday is the Sabbath.

Chapter 4

The Sinfulness Of Slavery

"The powers of hell are working with all their ingenuity to prevent the proc-lamation of the last message to the colored people." Testimonies for the Church, Vol. 6, pp. 7, 8.

When the Roman empire rose to world dominance, Blacks continued to keep the Sabbath. When the entire European Christian world accepted Sunday as the day of worship to the Almighty God, Blacks in Ethiopia kept the seventh-day Sabbath in accordance with the teachings of the Scriptures.

Africans began to lose sight of God with the arrival of explorers and of Christians fleeing the wrath of the Roman government. Portuguese sailors discovered the African continent in their search for adventure. Crusaders and exploiters descended upon this vast land, bringing with them aggression, war, exploitation, the slave trade and colonialism. Ethiopians were still keeping the Sabbath when the African slave trade began in 1441 with the assistance of King Nzinga, a Nkouwou, who was ruler in Angola.

The devil was very angry with the African people for keeping alive the Sabbath institution which affirms the Lord as Creator of all things, as Deliverer of mankind from the penalties of sin and as the One who upholds the entire universe. The devil does not want Black people to be saved eternally. In *Testimonies for the Church*, Vol. 9, p. 208, Ellen G. White states, "The powers of hell are working with all their ingenuity to prevent the proclamation of the last message to the colored people." So when Portuguese sailors visited Africa seeking to exchange trinkets for human labor, Blacks were sold into servitude by their own people.

The *Encyclopedia Britannica* defines slavery as "a societal institution based on ownership, dominance and exploitation of one human being by another and reciprocal submission on the part of the person owned. The owner may exact work or other services without pay and virtually without restriction and can deny the slave freedom of activity and mobility. Members of a family can be separated at the will of the owner, and marriages generally require the owner's permission. A slave is commonly regarded as an article of property, or chattel, and therefore can be sold or given away. Slaves do not come under the jurisdiction and laws that protect citizens, although special regulations may stipulate their treatment and behavior.

"Slavery has appeared almost universally throughout history among people of every level of material culture—from ancient Greece or the United States in the 19th century to various African and American Indian societies. Slavery is not unique to any particular type of economy. It existed among nomadic pastoralists of Asia, hunting societies of North American Indians, and traditionally served differing functions in these societies. Among agriculturists, where production led to material and cultural advancement, slaves were valued primarily as the major work force in production. Such societies are sometimes referred to as commercial slave societies, exemplified by the Roman Empire and the Old South of the United States, distinguishing them from slave-owning societies, in which slaves were principally for personal and domestic service, including concubinage. The latter type of slavery traditionally existed in parts of the Middle East, Africa and China. The more sophisticated agricultural societies, however, were able to use slaves most effectively, and in such societies slavery became systematic and highly institutionalized."—Encyclopedia Britannica, Vol. 20.

Slavery can be traced even further back to the Garden of Eden where Adam and Eve submitted themselves to Satan's domination by their disobedience to God. However, the Lord promised that the fallen pair would not be compelled to live as slaves throughout eternity. Jesus would come to set the captives free from enslavement, as well as from the penalty and the curse of sin.

Joseph's brothers, the sons of Jacob, sold him into slavery because of jealousy. But God intervened to see Joseph rise to the position of second in command in Pharaoh's realm, and his brothers' evil plan was turned into a blessing for saving the entire family. The Most High always rules in the affairs of men.

When the children of Israel were in the wilderness, a person could sell himself into bondage to pay his bills, etc. However, after a seven-year period, he was automatically set free; after forty-nine years, the entire camp was declared free from any encumbrances or indebtedness. The fiftieth year was known as the year of jubilee. During the early days of settling in the United States, many Europeans sold themselves into slavery as indentured servants in order to get to America. When their obligation was paid, they were set free.

"Slavery in Spain and Portugal, long an established institution, had continued throughout the Middle Ages, and the discovery of the New World in the 15th century created an unprecedented demand there for human labor. The demand was temporarily satisfied by the virtual enslavement of whole indigenous Indian populations from Peru to Central and Mexico. The Spanish conquistador Hernando Cortes in the early 16th century commented on the vast number of Indian slaves gathered and sold in the Mexican capital. The forced labor systems of encomienda and repartimiento instituted by the Hispanic colonists proved neither practical nor satisfactory, however. The Spanish soon found that the Indians, by reason of physique, tradition, and susceptibility to European diseases, were not ideal slaves. Also, being in their own familiar homeland, escape or revolt was relatively easy....

FORMER AMERICAN SLAVES

Sojourner Truth

Dred Scott

Robert (Doc) and Martha Talley

Albert and Gentry Talley

Nathan Talley

John Talley

"Indigenous people were pursued far into the jungles of the interior, captured and barbarously treated. As the Indian population diminished under these terrible conditions, slaves brought from Africa replaced them. Thus the slave trade in the New World, with its ever-increasing markets, rapidly expanded into an enormous and highly lucrative industry."—Encyclopedia Britannica, Vol. 20.

The practice of selling African labor to the Europeans, begun by Nzinga the Angolan king/queen in 1441, was continued by her son Alfonso. (It is believed that Nzinga was really a woman disguised as a man because the African culture at that time would not allow a female monarch.) Alfonso had several objectives in mind: to convert his people to Catholicism, the religion he had adopted; to benefit from the technological knowledge of the Europeans; and to control the rapacious appetite of the Portuguese for riches and especially for slaves, whom they sold in the New World.

What actually happened during this time is told by Cyrian Davis in his book *The History of Black Catholics in the United States*:

"In one bitter letter to the king (King Manuel I of Portugal), Alfonso expressed his disappointment regarding some of the Portuguese clergy who had been sent to evangelize the people. The king had sent a group of canons regularly from Lisbon.... After their arrival in the kingdom of Alfonso, they ceased to live the common life, began to live in concubinage with the women of the country, and started to traffic in slaves.... In the end, slavery meant the undoing of all that Alfonso had tried to accomplish. It must be admitted that Alfonso had agreed from the beginning to supply slaves as part of the regular trade agreement. Slavery was found in practically all of the African civilizations. The African form of slavery resulted primarily from being captured in war or being punished for crimes. It might be said in Alfonso's behalf that he probably did not know that slavery in Portugal meant something other than the kind of slavery found in Africa. The king soon found out that the appetite for slaves was insatiable. He found out that nothing would stop the Portuguese from expanding the slave trade, even if it meant seizing Alfonso's own people, and even members of his family. In fact, the king of Portugal made clear to him that slavery, like a narcotic, sucked every party into its corruption....

"Thus, at the very time when the Catholic Church was losing northern Europe to Protestant reform, an African king had wished to win his people to that same church. It was the curse of the slave trade that drove many of Alfonso's subjects against the church after his death in 1543."—*The History of Black Catholics in the United States*, p. 18.

When other European nations discovered this profitable venture, the enslavement of African people became a universal practice. Traders began to deliver human cargo to the Caribbean, South America and the rest of the New

World. The practice was introduced in the Caribbean more than two hundred years before it reached mainland America.

"The first slaves to arrive in the English colonies in America, about 20 in number, were put ashore at Jamestown, Virginia, in 1619. At that time the Africans were classed with White indentured servants brought from England under work contracts. Decades passed before Blacks in any significant number were brought to the colonies; in the main, they replaced escaped or freed indentured servants."—*Encyclopedia Britannica*, Vol. 20.

In his book *Before the Mayflower*, Lerone Bennett, Jr., gives this account of how slavery got started in the United States:

"She came out of a violent storm with a story no one believed, a name no one recorded and a past no one investigated. She was manned by pirates and thieves. Her captain was a mystery man name Jope, her pilot an English-man named Marmaduke, her cargo an assortment of Africans with sonorous Spanish names—Anthony, Isabella, Pedro.

"A year before the arrival of the celebrated 'Mayflower,' 113 years before the birth of George Washington, 244 years before the signing of the Emancipation Proclamation, this ship sailed into the harbor at Jamestown, Virginia, and dropped anchor into the muddy waters of history. It was clear to the men who received this 'Dutch man of War' that she was no ordinary vessel. What seems unusual today is that no one sensed how extraordinary she really was. Few ships, before or since, have unloaded a more momentous cargo.

"From whence did this ship come?

"From somewhere on the high seas where she robbed a Spanish vessel of a cargo of Africans bound to the West Indies.

"Why did she stop at Jamestown, the first permanent English settlement in America?

"No one knows for sure. The captain 'p'tended,' John Rolfe noted, that he was in great need of food; he offered to exchange his human cargo for 'vitualle.' The deal was arranged. Anthony, Isabella, Pedro, and 17 other Africans stepped ashore in August, 1619. The history of the Negro in America began."—*Before the Mayflower*, pp. 29, 30.

"Although slaves would seem to be a primitive source of energy that would lose importance with the advance of mechanization, the opposite proved true in the United States; the cotton gin, which came into use after 1800, prepared cotton for marketing so rapidly that the demand for slaves increased rather than decreased."—*Encyclopedia Britannica*, Vol. 20.

And so they came to the American shores, according to the old Negro spiritual: "Some through the water, some through the flood, some through the fire, but all through the blood. Some through great sorrow, but God gives His Son in the night seasons, and all the day long."

Forced into slavery against their will, our enslaved African forefathers yearned to be free. They often sang of a year of freedom, but it was not the intentions of the slave masters ever to set their unwilling African captives free. Deliverance did not come until 1863 with the signing of the Emancipation Proclamation by President Abraham Lincoln.

Chapter 5

All Night, All Day, Angels Keep Watching Over Me

"The angel of the Lord encampeth round about them that fear him, and delivereth them." Psalm 34:7

The institution of slavery robbed the Black man of many things, including the following:

(1) A place to call home—He was brought from his African shores by force. The family was destroyed and upon reaching the New World, he was not allowed to live on the same plantation with another slave from his own tribe. The lack of fellowship made life very lonely. His feeling of neglect found expression in the song, "Sometimes I feel like a motherless child, a long way from home."

(2) Dignity and self-worth—He was introduced to alcoholism; his will was broken; his sense of pride was taken; and he was subjected to poverty and indecent living. It was then that he sang, "Po' me, trouble will bear me down."

(3) Social status and morality—Immorality, which he was unaccustomed to, was thrust upon him. Africans were morally pure people. The home unit was broken and family members separated and sent to distant plantations, thus giving rise to a number of fatherless and motherless children. Being exposed to favoritism and intimidation, he lost respect even for his own people. When freedom finally came, the great poet Paul Lawrence Dunbar sought to rejuvenate the race with his poem, "Be proud, my race; be proud!"

(4) His health—He had to spend long hours in the field under the scorching sun, where he learned to eat almost anything in order to survive. His diet affected his physical, as well as his mental health. He suffered heart ailments, strokes and afflictions. His only hope of getting through the storm was his complete trust in Jesus; thus he began to sing, "I woke up this morning with my mind stayed on Jesus."

(5) The opportunity to learn—He was kept in ignorance by laws that denied him the right to learn to read, to write or to count in order to transact business for himself and his family. There were no schools for the slaves, and anyone caught teaching them could be arrested, fined, or imprisoned. It was the plan to keep the Black man in ignorance, but he heard someone read from the Bible that if anyone lacked wisdom, let him ask of God. He asked of God in faith and could later sing, "Jesus led me all the way."

(6) His worship—The religion of his homeland was characterized as heathen, demonic and superstitious in nature; thus, it was outlawed. The master was fearful of his slave's African religion and customs. The things the slave cherished were supplanted or replaced by the religion of the master. This

practice was used to keep slaves subdued and subjugated. As mentioned in an earlier chapter, the prophetess Ellen G. White wrote that the people of Ethiopia (Africa) kept the true Sabbath of the Bible as it had been kept from the fourth century. It is incomprehensible that these people should be considered heathens. While observing the deeds of his master, the slave could still sing, "Give me that ole time religion. It's good enough for me. Makes me love everybody. It will do when the world's on fire. It's good enough for me."

(7) His name—He was given another name so that he could not be located by his African name. He became an invisible person without existence, except to those who kept alive the institution of slavery.

Names are very symbolic and very meaningful in the various African cultures. When in Africa some years ago, I was introduced to a pastor in Rwanda whose name was "Simbeba." He was born while his parents were exiled in Zaire due to the tribal unrest in their own homeland. On returning to Rwanda, they told the border guards that the little boy's name was "Simbeba," meaning "he's just a little rat." They were permitted to take him back home with them, and the name stuck.

Africans are proud of their names. Alex Haley portrays this vividly in his book *Roots* as he related the story of Kintekunte's insistence on retaining his African name in America. His name then became "Boy" and his plantation name became Toby.

In America, a slave was identified by the name of the slave master on whose plantation he lived and worked. If sold to another master, another name change could, and usually did, take place. He was constantly frustrated regarding who he really was. In thinking about going to his heavenly home, he would sing, "There's a new name written down in glory, and it's mine."

The yoke of slavery weighed heavily on the transplanted Africans; the stripes that were placed upon them were harsh and severe. They were brought to ports of entry in America and placed on the auction block. One such auction block can still be seen on the corner of Auction and Main streets in Memphis, Tennessee.

Before the auction, they were subjected to an inspection process. Sound teeth suggested good health. Stripes on the back denoted that the slave had a rebellious history; a determined spirit and a made-up mind indicated that he had resisted slavery. Many scars on the back signaled trouble for the slave owner.

The lives of the slaves were wrought with hardship as they labored for the good of the master. Yet, little is found in the history books about Blacks in America or about their contributions to the development of the land, the religions and the churches of this country. They seem to have been "invisible people," whose good deeds, achievements and contributions were blotted out of the pages of history.

In an effort to keep them subdued, slave masters would invite slave preachers to speak to the slaves. The owners felt that the words from the Bible had a calming effect on their captives. They did, but the biblical teachings also placed within their hearts a longing to be free and prayers to God that He would send His angels to set them free.

They learned of Moses who brought deliverance to God's people when they were in Egyptian bondage under Pharaoh. Often they reflected on the deliverance of Daniel from the den of lions by the angel of God. They took comfort in the fact that angels were constantly watching over them. On the plantation, in the master's house, in the fields or wherever they eventually were taken to labor, they experienced the protection and felt the presence of angels.

The angels were ministering spirits that were sent forth to minister unto those who would be heirs of salvation. The slaves developed a relationship with God through the ministry of the angels. The first prayer taught to most African-American children by their parents was: "Now, I lay me down to sleep, the angels keep watching over me; I pray the Lord my soul to keep, the angels keep watching over me." They had faith to believe that angels would bring deliverance from enslavement, and the Lord used the angels to work in their behalf as He had done many times for His people through the ages. In hopes for their own deliverance from slavery, they often sang "Didn't my Lord deliver Daniel, then why not deliver po' me?"

Students who attended Oakwood College in Huntsville, Alabama, in the early days may remember Papa Moore, an ex-slave, who would relate how the slaves often could feel the presence of angels with them, especially when they were experiencing harsh trials from their owners. The experience was common across the land, and one of the traditional songs that they sang was "All night, all day, the angels keep watching over me."

The slaves learned about the work of angels on behalf of men. Since the days of Abraham, the Scriptures speak of angels interceding and protecting those on earth who desired to be led by God. These angels sent from glory, at times accompanied by the Son of God himself appearing as an angel—the highest archangel in glory—often came to earth to work on man's behalf. Long before He died on Golgotha's Hill, called Calvary, Jesus visited with men on earth. The Scriptures tell how two angels in the form of men at times accompanied Him. Angels were with Him when He visited with Abraham and Lot. Angels spoke to Isaac and Jacob.

When Jesus was born in Bethlehem, angels were present. They watched over Him when Mary and Joseph carried Him into Africa as they fled the wrath of Herod. They were present with Him in the mountain when the devil sought to tempt Him. They were at the cross when He died. They were at the tomb when He arose on Easter Sunday morning.

The angel Gabriel descended from heaven at the command of the Father, rolled back the stone that was before the sepulchre, and then sat on it and defied the observers to try to put it back. That mighty angel was heard at the tomb saying, "Thy Father calls Thee." Immediately, the Saviour came forth from the grave by the life that was in Himself. When He arose, the angels were there. The angels in heaven shouted for joy. Dr. Luke states in his gospel that two men informed the disciples at the empty tomb: "He is not here. He is risen." Luke 24:1.

Angels returned to glory with Him when He ascended from the Mount of Olives on a pillar of cloud. When the cloud received Him out of sight, the two men (angels) who had been with Him all through His days on earth assured the disciples that this same Jesus would come again in like manner as they had seen Him go into heaven. The ministry of the angels was significant for the carrying out of the mission of Christ on earth and for giving to Him safe conduct back to glory.

The teaching that Philip gave to the Ethiopian eunuch was attended by an angel. "And the angel of the Lord spake unto Philip, saying, Arise, and go toward the south unto the way that goeth down from Jerusalem unto Gaza, which is desert....

"And he arose and went: and, behold, a man of Ethiopia, an eunuch of great authority under Candace queen of the Ethiopians, who had the charge of all her treasure, and had come to Jerusalem for to worship, was returning home, and sitting in his chariot read Esaias, the prophet.

"Then the Spirit said unto Philip, Go near, and join thyself to this chariot. And Philip ran thither to him, and heard him read the prophet Esaias, and said, Understandest thou what thou readest? And he said, how can I except some man should guide me? And he desired Philip that he would come up and sit with him.

"And as they went on their way, they came unto a certain water: and the eunuch said, See, here is water; what doth hinder me to be baptized?

"And Philip said, If thou believest with all thine heart, thou mayest. And he answered and said, I believe that Jesus Christ is the Son of God." Acts 8:26–31, 36, 37.

Incidentally, the biblical beliefs of the Seventh-day Adventist Church today are essentially the same as those that the African believed when he returned to his homeland. He returned to his homeland and taught his people the things that he had learned while in Jerusalem and on his journey home. He had learned: (1) Psalms 100:3, "Know ye that the Lord is God. It is He that hath made us and not we ourselves." (2) Exodus 20:8–11, "Remember the Sabbath day to keep it holy...the seventh day is the Sabbath of the Lord, thy God." (3) Isaiah 58:13, "If thou turn away thy foot from the sabbath, from doing thy pleasure on my holy day; and call the sabbath a delight..." (4) John

14:3, "I will come again and receive you unto myself, that where I am, there ye may be also."

The Bible teaches that Jesus will come again to earth, attended by angels, for all of His believers. The angels led the eunuch back to Africa to tell the story to his people. The gospel of Jesus Christ has been preserved among the African people since 31 A.D. and since that time has spread to the ends of the earth. Angels will return with Christ when He bursts the clouds asunder and comes to earth to receive His church.

The next several chapters deal primarily with the historical and social perspective that formed the background for the chain of events that occurred in the religious world during the early and mid 19th century. This information is essential to an accurate understanding of the social and religious climate of the day and why things happened the way they did.

Chapter 6

Colored (Miracle) People

"God…hath made of one blood all nations of men for to dwell on all the face of the earth…" Acts 17:24–26

Mixing of the African and European races began virtually at the same time slavery began. While the slaves were being transported from Africa to the New World, the sea captains and crew members would engage in sexual intercourse with the women at sea. One such perpetrator was purported to have been a sea captain named John Newton[4] (1725–1807) who later became a preacher and the writer of the much sung hymn "Amazing Grace."

When the slave trade was outlawed in America in 1808, many slave holders who depended upon this labor to pick cotton, cut cane and stem tobacco suffered economic chaos. Many had to plant and harvest their own crops and resented working beside their own slaves in the field. Some owners became poverty stricken and took jobs as taskmasters on other plantations.

Inasmuch as slaves could no longer be imported legally, some owners instituted an alternate plan of producing more slaves through those they already owned. Masters began sleeping with the slave women to produce more children. This practice continued for decades. Many times the master would leave his shoes on the steps for the Black woman to polish, and in exchange for his sexual gratification, he would provide her food to feed her family. In other instances, the Black woman would be taken over by the slave owner; nothing was said, or could be said, for she was considered his property. Female slaves were used principally for personal and domestic service, including concubinage. Immorality was thrust upon them against their will.

"Grandpa" Haywood Moore, born a slave on the Jacob's plantation near Huntsville, Alabama, related many of his experiences to us who were students at Oakwood College during the 1930s and 1940s. He often told how the master would send the male slaves to the fields to work with a lash on the back and then would spend time in sexual activity with his (the slave's) woman.

One recorded incident took place in the state of Missouri. After repeatedly being subjected to the sexual abuses of her master, a slave girl named Celia killed him and destroyed his remains. He just seemed to have disappeared

---

4   Newton later repented of his sinful ways, gave his heart to the Lord and sought to make amends for his past deeds. It was in gratitude to God for his deliverance that he penned the words to "Amazing Grace."

one night, but suspicions in the community soon led to an investigation which pointed to Celia as the perpetrator of the crime. Although the sentiments among many Whites were in her favor, a decision had to be made whether to try her as a human being or as chattel. She was tried as chattel and hanged.

To have tried her as a human being would have upset the entire slave system of the nation. Many of the religious leaders of the South could not bring themselves to make a decision between their religion and their politics. These same feelings would haunt Adventist believers when they officially established the denomination near the end of the century.

While the sexual abuse of slave women produced the additional slaves the master wanted or needed, the conditions led to anger, resentment, revolts, killings and an increased desire on the part of the slaves to escape the abusive practices of the master. Winds of change and defiance swept across the land. Slaves began to run away from the plantations. Some were captured and returned to their masters. Often when a slave was planning to run away, the group would begin singing, "Steal away to Jesus. I ain't got long to stay here," or "One of these days, it won't be long, you gonna look for me, and I'll be gone!" The master enjoyed listening to the singing of what he thought were contented slaves when, in reality, they were distraught, angry and planning to escape.

The Fugitive Slave Laws were passed in 1850 in an effort to help slave owners hold on to their slaves, but the die had been cast. Freedom was in their bones. Every possible effort within their beings was exercised in an attempt to rid themselves of the rigors of this dehumanizing system. Concerning the Fugitive Slave Laws, Ellen White stated that the members of the Seventh-day Adventist group were to disregard them and engage in civil disobedience whatever the consequences.

By the turn of the 19th century, almost 40 percent of the slaves in America were the result of mixed relationships between master and slave. This different kind of slave in the house or in the field was described as "colored" (mixed-blood). The others were known as "darkies" or "Nubians," an African term for "Black." Everyone knew that the master was having children by his African slave and often by his own offspring. There were different groups of coloreds, yet all were slaves.

When Huey P. Long was governor of Louisiana, it is purported that he said to his fellow legislators during one of the sessions of the state legislature that he could take fifty cents' worth of hamburger meat and feed every pure-blooded White person in the state. In later years, his brother Earl became governor and told the legislature that everyone knew that the Longs had two families, one at home and the other across the railroad track. He was later placed in a mental institution.

With the mixing of the races, there came categorizing of the groups based on the percentage of African (Negro) blood present in their veins. Hatred and resentment began to be felt among the different people. The Negro was the most disdained of all. It was said that a Negro could be colored, but that a colored was not a Negro.

The categories that existed were: (1) Mulatto—The first generation offspring of an African and a White; a person of mixed European and African ancestry was half Black or half White, depending upon one's point of view. When slave women gave birth to the master's children, the children were mulattos or colored. (2) Quadroon—The offspring of a mulatto and a White, or a person who had one mulatto and one White parent. When mulatto girls reached young womanhood, the master would engage in sexual relationships with them to produce quadroons, who had one-quarter African blood. (3) Octoroon—An octoroon had one-eighth African blood, was the offspring of a quadroon and a White person, and had one African grandparent. By the time the relationship reached the octoroon child, the offspring usually could not be distinguished as having any strains of Negro blood and could easily slip to the White side of the family. Many did and enjoyed the advantages of being on that side of the family. Some held political offices. Some were well respected citizens in White social, business and religious circles, a status denied the Negro.

Other people of mixed ancestry involving Africans included the following: (1) The African-Indian, known also as Afro-Indians. Lerone Bennett, author of *Before the Mayflower*, establishes the fact that in 1444 A.D., Blacks were deposited in the New World by Dutch sailors; thus, when Christopher Columbus docked in the New World in 1492 with his Negro navigator Alonzo Nino[5] of the Nina, Africans were already here living with the Indians. From this association came a people known as African-Indians. These people were well acquainted with the land and were blood brothers of the Africans who were later brought to the New World as slaves.

(2) The African-Asians—In 1848 the Chinese people began coming to America to take advantage of the gold rush on the West Coast. However, their claims were denied them by the settlers, and most of them ended up as cooks and laundry operators. Many were sent South to pick cotton, but they refused to allow themselves to be used in that manner. Those who remained in the South became a part of the community, and in time some children with mixed African and Asian heritage were born.

The native American was really the descendant of Asians who in 1000 A.D. journeyed through the Bering Straits to the New World. They later

---

5   See the Negro Pilgrimage in America, by C. Eric Lincoln.

46

MULATTO AND CREOLE PEOPLE OF MIXED BLOOD

PRESENT DAY COLORED PEOPLE
FROM VARIOUS INDIAN TRIBES

became known as Indians. They considered themselves a distinct nation in the New World.

(3) There were people of other ethnic backgrounds living in America. Among them were the Creoles and the Nanticokes and Moors. *Encyclopedia Britannica* describes a Creole as "a descendant of French and Spanish settlers of the Gulf states, Louisiana, Mississippi, Alabama, Florida."

The Delaware mixed-blood groups might be mistaken for Blacks by some who do not understand their background, even though they may not have a drop of Negro blood in their veins. Indeed, prior to 1831, three official races of people lived in Delaware—the Negroes, the Whites and the Indians. However, after a court ruling involving an Indian named Levin Sockum and a person of mixed blood named Isaiah Harmon, Delaware passed a law that Indians and persons of mixed ancestry were Negroes. Ellen Gould Harmon White is said to have been related to these people.

Many of those affected by the law moved north into Pennsylvania, New York, New England and Canada. However, descendants of the Nanticoke Indians and the Moors who came from Algeria and Morocco in North Africa continued to pursue the ruling for years until, finally, another ruling was made in 1855 that there was a race of people who were not White nor Negroid, but "colored." Years later African-Americans were also called colored. This attitude on pigmentation in later years probably led to the establishment of the Colored Methodist Episcopal Church in 1870 in Jackson, Tennessee.

The Moors of southern Delaware who lived in Cheswold of Indian River Hundred insisted that they were coloreds and not Negroes, and they observed certain restrictions laid down by custom for colored people. These people traced their ancestry back to 1614 when John Rolfe a Virginia planter and the Indian maiden Pocahontas, who later adopted the Christian name Rebecca, were married.

Writing about these people, C.A. Weslager states the following in his *Delaware's Forgotten Folk*:

"The Cheswold Moors represent a settlement of mixed-bloods from other parts of the Delmarva Peninsula, and the colony soon became a melting pot of Indian descendants. As the population of the colony grew, a nationalism developed, and there came into existence a feeling that all must shun intermarriage with Negroes to preserve that nationalism. As a consequence they married among themselves…some of these people had darker skin which may have been due to earlier African infusion with the Indian or White stock. In others, it may have been the result of French, Moorish, and Spanish admixture with the native Indians. They are today neither pure Indians, pure Whites, nor Negroes. They must be accepted as a 'third race' which evolved from the intimate association of primary racial stocks during the era of American colonization. In seeking for a word to describe themselves, the term 'Moor' found in their folklore seemed adequate, and so it stuck."

This group included some well-known names such as the Streets, Hills, Norwoods, Johnsons, Burtons, Clarks, Cokers, Harmons, Morrises, Morgans, Seeneys and Warwicks (Warnicks). Some of these were members of the Seventh-day Adventist Church.

The mixed-blood epidemic in America became a grave concern for the nation. More than 40 percent of the slaves were of mixed ancestry. Their master fathers loved them and did not want to see them grow up in the environment of slavery; thus in 1822, Thomas Buchanan (cousin of President-to-be James Buchanan) went to the African continent to find a suitable place where these children could live as free people. The country of Liberia[6] was established for this purpose, and many of the children of mixed African and European parentage, including one thought to be the son of Abraham Lincoln, settled there. They took control, became the leaders of the government and, reportedly, began to practice the same type of oppression that was practiced on them in America.

While many of the children of mixed parentage returned to the African land of their mothers, grandmothers, or great grandmothers, a large number of them remained in America and began to have an impact on the political, religious, and social climate of the day. The ancestral ties to Africa of a number of these lighter-skinned contributors have not always been evident, and in many cases, conscious effort to obscure these ties has taken place. However, various authors have exposed a number of these closely guarded secrets.

J. A. Rogers, a Florida historian quoted *FACT*, a publication which he termed as the most outspoken of the big magazines, as stating in 1964 that there had already been a Black president of the United States, naming Warren G. Harding. In addition, he listed three other presidents—Thomas Jefferson, Andrew Jackson and Abraham Lincoln—as having Negro ancestry and intimated that there was another, whom he did not name. He also named Alexander Hamilton, who was from the Virgin Islands and became the first secretary of the treasury under George Washington, as well as Hannibal Hamlin, vice

---

6   "Liberia is the oldest independent Black nation in Africa and the second oldest in the world. Only Haiti is older. It became independent more than 110 years before any other country in tropical Africa. Although this government was founded by an American charitable society to provide a home for freed Black slaves from America, it was not recognized as a government by America until 1862. Aid from the United States helped these settlers resist both European colonial powers and opposition from Africans. Liberian settlers issued their Declaration of Independence in 1847."—Encyclopedia Britannica - 1968.

president under Abraham Lincoln, as having Black blood. Dr. Auset Bakufu in his book *The Six Black Presidents* names Dwight D. Eisenhower as being another Black president.

There were other persons of African or mixed ancestry who were important contributors to the social and religious activities of this period. Among them were Frederick Douglass, Hazen Foss, William Foye, Robert (Doc) Talley, Nathan Turner and Henry Highland Garnett. Their contributions, along with those of others, are listed in a subsequent chapter.

Still, the African in America, although mixed with many different ethnic groups, has always been placed at the bottom of the social, political and religious spectrum. Even his mixed-blood relatives began to despise him, leading to the practice among his own people of distinctions based on pigmentation. There developed expressions in the Black community such as, "If you are White, you are alright; if you are brown, stick around; but if you are Black, get back." People resented being called Black, and many fights resulted because of that.

Hundreds of years later, during the Civil Rights Movement of the 1960s, colored, Negroes, African-Americans and people of various mixed parentage came to the realization that they had more in common than not and that they all were victims of a corrupt and prejudicial society. Thus, the word "Black" became an endearing term.

"Black is beautiful! How beautiful it is to be Black!"

Chapter 7
Slave Revolts And The Abolitionist Movement
"Freedom is never volunteered by the oppressor; it must be demanded by the oppressed!"—Martin Luther King, Jr.

The late Martin Luther King, Jr., once said, "Freedom is never volunteered by the oppressor; it must be demanded by the oppressed." The slaves kept up their demand for freedom. From the beginning of the slave trade, an intense longing for freedom was in the hearts of the slaves. Many escaped from their masters. Some committed suicide rather than continue living under such circumstances. Some parents took the lives of their children rather than have them suffer under the vestiges and cruelties of slavery. Some kept insurrections stirred up everywhere. Some continued to seek the Lord.

Newspaper accounts told of Joseph Cinque, a captive from Sierra Leone who, with 52 other young Africans, was chained in the bottom of the ship, named Amistead, and taken to Havana, Cuba. Determined to be free, Cinque, of African royalty, organized followers while still at sea on the way to America. He killed the captain and officers of the ship and demanded that those who were left turn the ship around and return the captives to their homeland, but the slave dealers steered the rebels to a port in Connecticut and had them arrested. With public sentiment in their favor, the courts exonerated them and returned them to their homeland.

The songs the slaves sang while in slavery often expressed their desire for freedom. They could be heard singing, "And before I'll be a slave, I'll be buried in my grave and go home to my Lord and be free!" Many escaped from their enslavement, sometimes teaming up with the Indians, hiding in the swamps by day and destroying the master's property by night. They kept constant fear in the hearts of their owners with their attempts at freedom.

Despite their many attempts, slaves have not always been credited with doing much to protest their enslavement and win their freedom. Fact is that there were at least 109 slave revolts that occurred on land between 1663 and 1864 and 55 that occurred at sea from 1699 to 1845.

The Quakers launched the first organized opposition to slavery in America as early as 1724, declaring that the institution was wrong, immoral and sinful. They, along with the Methodists, were sympathetic to the plight of the slaves and outlawed it among their members. The groundswell led to the development of a group that became known as "abolitionists" who actively worked to end slavery. Christians who also expressed concerns about slavery, though less dedicated to its abolition, became known as "apologists."

Some of the leaders of the abolitionist movement were Federick Douglass, Harriet Tubman, Harriet Beecher Stowe, Henry Ward Beecher, William Still, William Lloyd Garrison, John Brown, Henry Highland Garnett, John Byington, Sojourner Truth, John P. Kellogg and many others. One of them, Harriet Beecher Stowe, the sister of the great Methodist preacher Henry Ward Beecher, realizing how inhumane slavery was, wrote a book entitled Uncle Tom's Cabin, which vividly painted the picture of the slaves' plight. Her book pricked the conscience of the nation and the world.

Before that, however, Gabriel Prosser and Jack Bowler were executed around the turn of the 19th century for leading slave revolts in Richmond, Virginia, and in 1822 Denmark Vessey of Charleston, South Carolina, was executed for planning a similar strategy. Of course, the importation of slaves had been banned since 1808, but the right to hold slaves was still upheld by the constitution.

This unrest was felt not only in America, but around the world where slavery was practiced, the desire for freedom fanned the flames of activism. In 1793 on the island of Haiti, a gallant, courageous mulatto named Toussaint l'Ouverture led his people in a revolt against the rulers and people of France. He brought liberation to his people and successfully led them to set up their own government.

Abolitionists William Wilberforce (for whom Wilberforce University in Ohio is named) and Thomas Clarkson were instrumental in getting the British Parliament to outlaw the slave trade in 1807. Spain and Portugal officially abolished trafficking in slaves in 1840.

In the 1830s Simon Bolivar, a creole, and his followers successfully fought for the freedom of the slaves in other parts of the West Indies and South America. Once again, the nations of Europe were made to withdraw their rulership from the New World and to set the captives free. The nationals took over the reins of government and began to run their own countries and determine their own destinies in Jamaica, Trinidad, Cuba, South America and in other islands and territories touched by the Caribbean Sea. However, with thoughts of freedom in the air throughout the Western Hemisphere, Blacks in North America saw little progress in that direction; they remained in bondage, but restless.

This restlessness spilled over into the church services on Sunday. The masters often felt that the slaves were enjoying the services, which, more often than not, they were; but in reality they were also in the balcony plotting how to escape the system. They were determined to free their bodies, souls and spirits. They became determined, dedicated, unrelenting Christians who thanked and served the Lord for bringing them through the trials of the week and sought His guidance in leading them to freedom.

REVOLUTIONISTS...

Joseph Cinque, African revolutionist—1839

Toussaint L'Ouverture, Haitian revolutionist— 1793

Nathan Turner, revolutionist—1831

...AND ABOLITIONISTS

Frederick Douglas, abolitionist

Rosetta (Douglas) Spragg—daughter of Frederick Douglas and member of the First Seventh-day Adventist Church of Washington, D.C.

William Still, spark of the Abolitionist Movement— great uncle of the late Josephine Roberts

Henry Highland Garnet, abolitionist Presbyterian minister

Sojourner Truth   *John Byington, first*   *Harriet Tubman,*
       president of the General *the Black Moses*
        Conference of SDAs

In 1831 Nathan Turner, an educated mulatto slave-turned-preacher living in Southampton, Virginia, led a slave rebellion throughout the countryside and killed a large number of White people—men, women and children. He stated that the Lord had told him to rise up and kill the enemy, whom he (Turner) identified as being any White person. He was captured and executed, but the rebellion placed fear in the hearts of White people across the land.

The state of Mississippi passed a law that no Negro (Black) man could be a preacher in the state. Delaware passed a law prohibiting non-residents from preaching within its borders and banning the sales of arms and munitions to Negroes. When these laws took effect, the Moor and Nanticoke people made it clear that they were not Negro, mulatto, nor White, but that they were descendants of Europeans and Indians. However, a court decision ruled that they were Negroes, leading many of them to move North to escape the stigma associated with the Nat Turner rebellion.

The Turner rebellion had an opposite effect on Blacks; it sparked a desire for freedom within the hearts of this captive people. However, it also brought some reluctance on the part of Black persons to preach the gospel because of the suspicion with which Whites now regarded Black preachers; some others refused to ignore what they saw as their call from the Lord to continue to preach the Word that all captives must be free. The courage Turner displayed soon spread throughout the New World.

The following is a list of some of the persons who were active in the social and religious issues of the day:

JAMES VARICK (1750–1827), Newburgh, New York. He was the founder of the African Methodist Zion Church in 1796 and later became its first bishop. He became a strong proponent for his people to return to Africa, the Motherland.

RICHARD ALLEN (1760–1831), Philadelphia, Pennsylvania. Rev. Richard Allen, along with Rev. Absalom Jones, withdrew from the St. George Methodist Church in 1787 to protest the unkind treatment and other restrictions placed upon worshipers of African descent. They established the African Methodist Church, now found throughout the world. Allen became its first bishop. One of his famous sayings was, "I do not care how dark the night may be, I'll always believe in the coming of the morning."

SOJOURNER TRUTH (1797–1883), Hurley, New York. One of the morning stars of the abolitionist movement in America was Sojourner Truth. She served under a farmer of Dutch descent named Johannes Hardenbergh and spoke Dutch until she was 12 years old. After mastering the English language she traveled widely throughout New England and the Midwest speaking out against the slave institution. Her deep voice, quick wit and inspiring faith helped to spread her fame.

Once, when Frederick Douglass despaired of hope for Blacks, she encouraged him from the back of the room with the words, "Fred, is God dead?" Often she met with Abraham Lincoln and gave moral support to him. Her speeches were based on her belief that people best show their love for God by their love and active concern for others. Originally named Isabella Baumforce, she changed her name to Sojourner Truth in 1843 to reflect the fact that she was a "sojourner looking for truth."

She lived during the time William Foye told his visions about the coming of the kingdom of heaven to earth, and she became an adherent of his teachings. Although Sojourner Truth was a staunch member of the Methodist Church, in her later years, she was baptized by Uriah Smith and became a member of the Seventh-day Adventist Church. She finally settled in Battle Creek, Michigan, where she spent her last days. Uriah Smith conducted her funeral at the Dime Tabernacle S. D.A. Church. She was buried in the Oak Hill Cemetery,[7] near the resting places of James and Ellen White and members of their family, John Harvey Kellogg and some of his family members, and Mr. C. W. Post, a rival of the Kellogg Corporation in the breakfast cereal business.

DRED SCOTT. The quest for freedom was in the heart of Dred Scott who in 1795 was owned by Captain Peter Blow and John Moore in Southampton, Virginia. In 1818 Scott was moved to Madison County, Alabama, where he served for 12 years on a plantation that would later be sold to Seventh-day Adventists for the establishment of Oakwood Training School, now Oakwood College.

---

7   Many pioneers of the Seventh-day Adventist Church are sleeping at Oak Hill in Battle Creek, Michigan. Among them are the Letts, the Seeneys and the Buckners.

After being transferred from Alabama to St. Louis, he filed a suit through the courts in Missouri in 1846 requesting that his freedom be granted on the grounds that he had been living in a free state (Wisconsin) before returning to Missouri. The courts denied the request.

FREDERICK DOUGLASS (1817–1895), Easton, Maryland. He was a product of race mixing during slavery. He became the leading spokesman for American Blacks in the 1800s. He was born a slave and became a noted author and speaker who devoted his life to the abolition of slavery and the fight for Black rights. He made many visits to the White House to speak with President Lincoln on behalf of his people and against the institution of slavery.

Frederick Augustus Washington Bailey was born in Tuckahoe, Maryland, near Easton. At the age of eight, he was sent to Baltimore to work for one of his master's relatives. There, helped by the wife of his new master, he began to educate himself. In 1838, the young man fled from his master and went to New Bedford, Massachusetts. To avoid capture, he dropped his two middle names and changed his last name to Douglass.

He listened to the teachings of William Foye but chose to remain a member of the African Methodist Episcopal Zion Church. Although he never became a member of the Seventh-day Adventist Church, which was established during his lifetime, his daughter Rosetta (Douglass) Spragg was a faithful member of the First SDA Church in Washington, D.C., where she remained for her entire lifetime.

ROBERT (DOC) TALLEY (1816–1900), Hennin, Tennessee. He was born a slave of mixed Irish and African heritage. His father was a lumberman of Irish-Canadian descent; his mother was African and had at least two children by the master of the house. He was my grandfather. My grandfather's sister, Aunt Drucilla, was a very fair-skinned woman who could have been mistaken for a White person. Grandma Talley was a Cherokee Indian whose ancestors were led on a death march from North Carolina and Virginia to Oklahoma. Thousands of her people died in transition. The story is told in the book entitled *Bury My Heart at Wounded Knee.*

The researcher, Alex Haley, in his books, *Roots, The Second Generation* and *Queen*, reveals how widespread the interrelationship of the races was throughout the South—Alabama, Arkansas, Georgia, Kentucky, Louisiana, Mississippi, Tennessee and Virginia—and even in some northern states.

In this lumbering town of Hennin in western Tennessee, about 50 miles north of Memphis, cotton was not king as it was elsewhere; lumber was king. Therefore, not too many slave hands were needed, and the relationship between the races (although undesirable) was not as strained as it was in other places. Grandpa Robert and Aunt Drucilla had privileges denied slaves elsewhere. They moved boldly in and out among the people. My sister Lucille recalls my mother saying that when freedom finally came, Grandpa Talley moved the family to Hickman, Kentucky, and purchased land to grow crops for the family. Many times the White people sought to take his land and put "For Sale" signs up on his property, but Grandpa would always tear them down.

WILLIAM FOYE (1817–1893), Augusta, Maine. Born free, he was a mulatto who was given visions from God of events that would change the thinking of the religious world during the 1840s. He was the first of three persons in the Advent Awakening to receive visions intended to strengthen the believers who would face the disappointment of 1844. Unlike Foss, another mulatto, who also had visions but refused to tell them, Foye revealed the visions and had them published in the newspaper in Gorham, Maine. That God is no respecter of persons was demonstrated in this servant whom He chose to bear the prophetic gift to the Adventist community. Dr. Delbert Baker in his book describes him as "the unknown prophet." Eunice Harmon and her afflicted daughter, Ellen, attended some of the meetings held by Foye in Beethoven Hall when Ellen was 16 years of age.

It is interesting that when the early church fathers wrote the history of the Advent Movement that Foye was not mentioned.

HAZEN FOSS (1819–1893), Portland, Maine. He received visions from the Lord but was reluctant to share them because of the law passed in Mississippi and supported by other states that forbade preaching by Blacks. Ellen G. White's sister Mary was married to his brother. Seventh-day Adventist historians say that Foss encouraged Ellen White to tell the visions that the Lord had shown her. *The Adventist Encyclopedia* states that Foss felt that he was lost because of his refusal to share with the people the visions that the Lord had given him.

HARRIET TUBMAN (1820–1913), Dorchester County, Maryland. Another courageous leader of the abolitionist movement was Harriet Tubman, who escaped from slavery in 1849. With gun in hand, she returned to the South and single-handedly carried more than 300 fellow slaves to freedom via the Underground Railroad[8] system of conducting slaves from home to home,

---

8   Whites and Blacks established this system of transporting slaves from the South to the North and onward to Canada and to freedom. Active in this group were William Still, whose grandniece Mrs. V. L. Roberts joined the S. D. A. Church; Frederick Douglass, whose daughter Mrs. Rosetta Spragg of Washington, D. C., also was an S. D. A. member; Bishop Morris Brown, founder of Morris Brown College in Atlanta; the White leader of the Raiders, John Brown, who died for the cause; John Harvey Kellogg of Battle Creek, Michigan; John Byington, the first president of the General Conference of Seventh-day Adventists; Harriet Tubman and Sojourner Truth.

CONTEMPORARY PROPHETS OF THE 1800s

Hazen Foss—1831

Ellen G. Harmon—1846

William Foye—1843

"station" to "station" and to eventual freedom in the North. Incidentally, James Byington, the first president of the General Conference of Seventh-day Adventists, was an abolitionist who sheltered many Blacks and Indians in his home on their way to freedom, and Pine Forge Academy in Pottstown, Pennsylvania, was one of the stops on the Underground Railroad.

CHARLES M. KINNEY (1855–1951), Richmond, Virginia. "The Morning Star of Black Adventism." "Although not one of the crusaders of the abolitionist movement, Kinney was a product of race-mixing during the days of slavery. After freedom came he worked his way to Reno, Nevada, where he attended evangelistic services conducted by J. N. Loughborough, accepted the Seventh-day Adventist faith, and later became the first Black member of the Reno, Nevada, church."—*S. D. A. Encyclopedia*, Vol. 12, p. 741.

Kinney became the first Black man to be ordained as a minister of the Seventh-day Adventist Church and became a champion for the rights and respect of his people in the church.

CHARLES ALBERT TINDLEY (1856–1933), Philadelphia, Pennsylvania. He was born a slave in 1856 and became a Methodist minister. Tindley introduced gospel hymns that had universal appeal to the human heart into the Black community. A number of his creations are still sung in churches today. Among them are: "Take Your Burden to the Lord and Leave It There," "Hallelujah! Hallelujah! The Storm is Passing Over," and "I'll Overcome Some Day," which became the freedom song "We Shall Overcome Some Day" during the Civil Rights Movement. He brought hope and trust to the hearts of many of his people through his preaching and singing.—*Songs of Zion*, pp. 4–6.

BOOKER T. WASHINGTON (1858–1915), Hale Ford, Virginia. In his book entitled *Up From Slavery*, p. 2, Washington states, "Of my father I know even less than of my mother. I do not even know his name. I have heard reports to the effect that he was a White man who lived on one of the nearby plantations. Whoever he was, I never heard of his taking the least interest in me or providing in any way for my rearing. But I do not find especial fault with him. He was simply another unfortunate victim of the institution which the Nation unhappily had engrafted upon it at the time."

TAZWELL B. BUCKNER (1860–1924), Vicksburg, Mississippi. Buckner was one of the first colored Seventh-day Adventist workers in the South. He and his wife, Amy, were fair-skinned people who escaped from hardship in Mississippi and settled in St. Louis, Missouri, to a life of comfort. Buckner, the first cousin of Etta Littlejohn[9] and Lizzie Kincaid was a descendant of mixed-race people (mulattos).

After his ordination in 1898, Buckner's ministry expanded into Alabama where he organized the work in Selma and Montgomery. The Fraziers, Fountains, Johnsons, Wesleys and others, who became pioneers of the church, joined through Buckner's ministry. He conducted evangelistic crusades in Talladega, as a result of which a public school teacher named Ann Evelyn McClellan, daughter of the famous Civil War leader General George Brinton McClellan, was baptized. Turner Battle II, a native Creole from Louisiana and a student[10] from the Huntsville Training School was Buckner's associate. He later married Miss McClellan, and they became the parents of Turner III, Ann and Maurice Tazwell Battle. Maurice was named for Tazwell Buckner and many years later would serve as associate secretary of the General Conference of Seventh-day Adventists.

Some of Buckner's children married into the Fred H. Seeney family of Nanticoke/Moor descent. Buckner died in Cheswold, Delaware after an extended illness and was eulogized by Pastor L. C. Sheafe, another son of the Delaware leaders.

Charles Bradford states that at one time when Elder Buckner was riding in the "Jim Crow" coach on the train, he was instructed by the conductor to move into the coach designated for White people. He responded, "You White folks have messed us up so until you don't know who we are!"

Buckner was the first colored person to serve as a member of the board of directors for the school for Blacks in Huntsville, now Oakwood College.

GEORGE WASHINGTON CARVER (1864–1943), Diamond, Missouri. Born during the slave era but after the signing of the Emancipation Proclamation, Carver grew up on a Missouri farm, where he developed a strong interest in plant life. He worked his way through high school and college, eventually receiving a master's degree in agriculture from Iowa State College

---

9   Etta Littlejohn was the mother of Charles E. Bradford, president emeritus of the North American Division of Seventh-day Adventists, and the grandmother of Calvin B. Rock, the senior vice president of the General Conference of Seventh-day Adventists.

10   Turner graduated from the Huntsville School in 1911, along with Benjamin W. Abney, Sr., who was among the first African-Americans to serve as a missionary for the church.

in 1896. That same year, he accepted a teaching post at Tuskegee Institute in Alabama and became director of the school's agricultural research program. Carver was a frequent dinner guest in the A. T. Maycock family home when the family lived near Tuskegee. Calvin E. Moseley, Jr., who later was the director of the Department of Religion at Oakwood College, was a student at Tuskegee when Carver was there. Moseley states that he gave his heart to God while attending one of Dr. Carver's Bible classes.

These are just a few Africans and African-Americans whom the Lord used to change the world.

Chapter 8

The Prophetess, Ellen Gould Harmon White

"Surely the Lord God will do nothing but he revealeth his secret unto his servants the prophets." Amos 3:7

Who was Ellen Gould (Harmon) White?

Ellen Gould Harmon was born in Gorham, Maine, November 26, 1827, to Robert and Eunice Harmon during the period of the mixed-blood child explosion. The question has been posed to officials of the E. G. White Estates at the General Conference of Seventh-day Adventists regarding the ethnic background of Ellen White, who is recognized as the prophetic voice to the Seventh-day Adventist Church. Only the paternal Harmon side of her ancestry has been disclosed, and that appears traceable to the "third race" of people designated by law in the courts of Delaware in 1831 and 1855. Although there has been silence concerning the maternal Gould side, it may be linked to the residents of the Gouldtown community in Bridgewater, New Jersey, who are descendants of the same "third race" of people.

Ellen's ethnicity has the appearance of a closely guarded secret; however, the book entitled *Delaware's Forgotten Folks*, tells of the Harmon family as having strains of mixed blood between the Nanticoke Indian tribe and the fair-skinned Moor people whose roots are in North Africa. It pointed to the Sockum, Harmon, Wright, Hill, Street, Morgan, Arties, Clark and Coker families as falling into this same mixed-blood category. Some of these people migrated northward from Delaware to Pennsylvania, Maine, upstate New York, Canada and westward. Milo Allison, a descendant of the Harmon and Seeney families, tells of Ellen's visits to the home of her colored cousins when she visited the city of Chicago.

It has been stated that a stone to Ellen's nose, tossed by a schoolmate, when she was nine years old disfigured her face. However, a picture of Ellen's twin sister reveals that both Ellen and her twin sister had identical features, leaving one to wonder whether it was the stone or the genes that were responsible for Ellen's features. Some have speculated that the stone may have been thrown because of the racial biases that existed against people of mixed blood in those days.

The late Jacob Justiss in his book *Ebony Angels*, p. 15, gives insight into the racial climate of that time by relating the experience of one man. He states, "Father Bowles, as he was called, because of his age when he joined with William Miller, had been born in Boston of illustrious parents, his father, an African servant and his mother (mulatto), the daughter of a famous Revolutionary Colonel Morgan. He...was instrumental in raising up many

…and her
husband,
James
E.
White

*James and Ellen and their children, J. Edson
and wife Emma and Willie C.*

Ellen G. White in vision

Ellen and her twin sister, Elizabeth

Ellen and sister, Mary

churches.… In keeping with the temper of the times, he was often menaced because he was a Black preacher. On one occasion, by his powerful preaching, he was able to turn the tables on a group. Some Whites had threatened to throw him into a baptismal pond. He ended up going into the water, but to baptize them."

Black members of the Seventh-day Adventist denomination have often questioned whether Ellen White was a member of the Negro race. There is reason to believe that there were no Negroes in her family roots, but there is evidence to suggest that there are members of the colored race, discussed in Chapter 6, in her ancestry.

Although there remains some unanswered questions about Ellen's ancestral history, much is known about racial conditions that existed during the time in which she lived. This was a time when a sizable number of people were crossing the color line to a new lifestyle of freedom. Andrew Jackson, Abraham Lincoln and Hannibal Hamlin were all contemporaries of Ellen Gould Harmon White; they were cited as persons who had strains of Negro blood but passed over and identified with the White side of their ancestry.

The Harmon family tree can be traced back to John Harmon, who was born in 1650 and died in 1742. John's great grandson Robert was the father of Ellen Gould Harmon. Isaac Harmon was named in a lawsuit in 1831 which resulted in a ruling by the courts in Delaware that the Harmons were of a third race of people designated as "Colored." The Gould family tree can be traced to John Gould whose granddaughter Eunice was the mother of Ellen Gould Harmon. However, in Bridgewater, New Jersey, which is not far from the Delaware border, there is an area of the city known as "Gouldtown" where only fair-skinned people live. Dark-skinned people do not live there.

Ellen and her twin sister Elizabeth were the last of eight children in the family. She was in her early teens when, along with members of her family, she accepted the biblical interpretations of the Baptist farmer-turned-preacher, William Miller. She and her mother had previously attended services held by William Foye in Beethoven Hall in Portland, Maine, in 1843. With Miller and 50,000 other Adventists, she suffered the bitter disappointment of October 22, 1844, when Jesus Christ did not return to earth for His church as expected.

In December 1844, about two months after "the great disappointment," God gave Ellen the first of an estimated 2,000 visions that she received during her lifetime. In August 1846, she married James E. White, a 25-year old Adventist minister of Palmyra, Maine. James shared Ellen's conviction that God had called her to do the work of a prophet. Soon after their marriage, James and Ellen began to keep the seventh-day Sabbath according to the fourth commandment of Exodus 20:8–11. They had been instructed about the Sabbath by Joseph Bates, an old sea captain, and by Rachel Oaks Preston, a member of the Seventh-day Baptist Church. This couple later became pioneers of the Seventh-day Adventist denomination.

James and Ellen had four sons—Herbert, Henry, Edson and William—two of whom died at an early age. Herbert died as an infant of a few weeks, and Henry died when he was 16 years old. Edson and William became Adventist ministers. Willie the youngest remained close to his mother's side and in later years became her spokesman. One of his children, Arthur, followed in his steps and became a teacher at Andrews University in Berrien Springs, Michigan, and was also unofficially accepted by the believers as the authority on the interpretations of Ellen's writings.

Edson was a maverick and for a while ventured from the family and the faith. He later returned and dedicated his life to ministering to the colored people in the southern part of the United States.

Ellen G. White was a prolific writer. She was in ill health most of her life. Notwithstanding, this frail child, after being instructed by God to give prophecies to the church and to the world, became a literary giant, the author of more than 60 books, as well as manuscripts, other documents and pamphlets that have helped the Seventh-day Adventist denomination to have a definite direction on the road to the kingdom of God. Beginning in 1851, when she published her first book, *Early Writings*, she produced a steady stream of articles, books and pamphlets. Of her scores of books, some are devotional in nature. Others are selections from the many personal letters of counsel she wrote over the years. Still others are historical, tracing the ongoing struggle between Christ and Satan for control of the minds, not only of individuals, but also of nations.

She published books on education, health, race relations and other topics of special significance to the church. Since her death, about 50 compilations have been produced in large part from previously unpublished writings. She also wrote several thousand articles that have been published over the years in the Review and Herald, *Signs of the Times* and other Seventh-day Adventist periodicals. Her book entitled, *The Desire of Ages* is among the many volumes in the Library of Congress.

Today's events seem to show that Ellen G. White was more than 100 years ahead of her time! The following comparisons with her prophecies support that fact;

* I WAS SHOWN . . .

1869: "Whatever disturbs the circulation of the electric currents in the nervous system lessens the strength of the vital powers, and the result is a deadening of the sensibilities of the mind."—*Education*, p. 209.

1934: "Minute electrical charges are vital to the functioning of the brain."— Dr. Charles Mayo of the Mayo Clinic.

* I WAS SHOWN...

1905: "People are continually eating flesh that is filled with tuberculosis and cancerous germs. Tuberculosis, cancer and fatal diseases are thus communicated."—*Counsels on Diet and Foods*, p. 388.

1956: "Many, if not all, malignant tumors may be caused by viruses (midget germs). Thus, a large number of malignant tumors of different morphology and in different species of animals could be transmitted from one host to another by filtered extracts."—Ludwick Grose, M.D., *Journal of American Medical Association*.

* I WAS SHOWN...

1905: "Tea and coffee do not nourish the system. Their effect is produced before there has been time for digestion and assimilation, and what seems to be strength is only nervous excitement. When the influences of the stimulant is gone, the unnatural forces abate, and the result is a corresponding degree of languor and debility."—*Counsels on Health*, p. 463.

1967: "Caffeinism is said to be current among intellectual workers, actresses, waitresses, nocturnal employees, and long distance automobile drivers. Illness otherwise unexplained may be caused by excessive ingestion of xanthine alkaloids, including those in coffee, tea, cocoa, and those popular beverages."— H. A. Riemann, *Journal of the American Medical Association*.

* I WAS SHOWN...

April 21, 1890: "The tempest is coming, and we must get ready for the fury by repentance toward God and faith toward our Lord Jesus Christ. The Lord will arise to shake terribly the earth. We shall see troubles on all sides. . . Fires will break out unexpectedly, and no human effort will be able to quench them. Palaces of earth will be swept away in the fury of the flames. Disaster by rail will become more and more frequent; confusion, collision and death without a moment's warning will occur on the great lines of travel."—*Testimonies for the Church*, Vol. 6, p. 408.

1997: These are events that take place each passing day.

* I WAS SHOWN...

1902: "Light has been given me that the cities will be filled with confusion, violence, and crime, and that these things will increase till the end of this earth's history."—*Testimonies for the Church*, Vol. 7, p. 84.

In a vision of Jesus' triumphant entry into glory after He came from Joseph's tomb, Ellen tells of the reception that took place before the Father, Holy Spirit, angels and beings from other worlds. Astronomers having developed powerful telescopes show galaxies that are millions of light years away coming into view. They are convinced that there are other intelligent beings in other parts of the universe. Ellen White, the prophetess, spoke of intelligent beings from other worlds that were at the counsel table when Jesus returned to His Father's side.

"All heaven was waiting to welcome the Saviour to the celestial courts. As He ascended, He led the way, and the multitudes of captives set free at His resurrection followed. The heavenly host, with shouts and acclamations of praise and celestial song, attended the joyous train....

"There is the throne, and around it the rainbow of promise. There are cherubim and seraphim. The commanders of the angel hosts, the sons of God, the representatives of the unfallen worlds, are assembled. The heavenly council before which Lucifer had accused God and His Son, the representatives of those sinless realms over which Satan had thought to establish his dominion, all are there to welcome the Redeemer. They are eager to celebrate His triumph and to glorify the King."—*Desire of Ages*, pp. 833, 834.

Ellen was a true prophet sent by God to direct people on their journey to the kingdom. Some in the Seventh-day Adventist Church seek to discredit her as one sent by God, but the prophecies that she revealed continue to come true.

During her lifetime, she wrote a number of articles concerning the church's duty to colored people. At one time she confessed that she would not live a coward and die one leaving her work undone. (*The Southern Work*, p. 10.) It was then that she began to write and to speak of the church's duty to the colored people of America—the offspring of White slave masters and their Black African slaves—whose children became colored and are found across the land even unto this day.

In later years, Ellen often spoke of the sinfulness and brutality of slavery. She expressed concern for the colored people and for the need to get the message of God's love to them before the Lord returns for His church. One of her final acts on behalf of this people was to dictate in her Last Will and testament that one-tenth of the net proceeds from her writings be used to advance the work among colored people in the southlands of the United States of America. When the terrible institution of slavery reached its peak, the Lord sent this prophetess into the world to help the pharaohs of earth to let His people go.

What was Ellen G. White's ethnicity? Or, does it really matter? The following quotation is taken from the book *Seventh-day Adventist Believe*:

"The Holy Spirit is the moving force behind church unity. Through Him believers are led to the church.... Calling them from every nationality and race, the Holy Spirit baptizes people into one body—the body of Christ, the church. As they grow into Christ, cultural differences are no longer divisive. The Holy Spirit breaks down barriers between high and low, rich and poor, male and female. Realizing that in God's sight they are equal, they hold one another in esteem."

It should not make a difference to adherents of the gospel what race Ellen was. The fulfillment of her visions and prophecies, her Negroid features, her concerns for the Christian treatment of the colored people and the helping hand she extended in their behalf tend to make one appreciate being affiliated with her.

The Lord God made of one blood all nations to dwell upon the earth (Acts 17:26). Adam and Eve were the first parents of the human race; thus, all are of the same parentage from creation. The Lord destroyed all creatures of earth at the time of the flood and began once again to repopulate the earth through Noah and his family. Genesis 11:1 states that "the whole earth was of one language, and of one speech." When another two thousand years passed, "God sent forth His Son, made of a woman, made under the law, to redeem them that were under the law, that we might receive the adoption of sons." Galatians 4:4.

The lineage of Christ in Matthew 1 reflects that the blood of all nations, kindreds and types of people flowed through the veins of Jesus Christ, the Saviour of the universe. It is highly possible that the blood of many nations (African, European, Indian, other) flowed through the veins of Ellen G. (Harmon) White .

Ellen Gould (Harmon) White's ethnic roots have no bearing on her connection with God and the guidance that He gave to her to help preserve a remnant of the church that Christ left on earth when He ascended to heaven. Such will have all of the characteristics of the early Christian church to which the disciples and apostles belonged. This people will adhere to the biblical teachings of God and give this gospel a certain sound to make ready a people to cross over into the heavenly Canaan land. She was a chosen vessel of God who lived in a specific era during which the African-Americans were brought from slavery to freedom. She played a specific role in the history and closing events of the Christian church.

In Seventh-day Adventist circles, she is spoken of as "the servant of the Lord." Her writings are referred to as the "Testimonies for the Church" or the "Spirit of Prophecy" (Revelation 19:10). She departed this life in 1915. As far as we know, she was the last of the prophets sent by God, and her testimonies and prophecies for the church are sufficient to guide us on our journey home.

Chapter 9

Religious Awakenings

*"Therefore, behold, I will …cause them to know, I will cause them to know
mine hand and my might; and they shall know that my name is the Lord."*
Jeremiah 16:21

From the earliest days of slavery, the church and service to God were the only harbingers to Black people that a better day was coming. Hope was inspired, release was envisioned and burdens were lightened in the church. Happiness and peace of mind could be found in the church house, for it was there that Black people found solace and consolation in being able to quietly "steal away to Jesus."

In the beginning, the slaves and masters worshiped together, but eventually slaves sought their own places of worship where they could laugh, sing their own songs, cry sometimes, shout their praises, clap their hands for joy, pat their feet to the beat of the music and talk back to the preacher—a place where they could vent their frustrations from the trials and struggles that had beset them during the week, a place where they could "have church." And they had church anywhere they found themselves, whether in a building, in the field while at work or just walking along the road and reflecting on God's goodness to them. Their spontaneous praise gave expression in "Thank you, Jesus. Thank you, Sir!"

Religion was the outlet that breathed tolerance into the struggles that the slaves encountered. Eventually, all of life became wrapped up in religion and the church. The religion of Jesus gave assurances of freedom. The sight of birds flying inspired the song, "Some bright morning when this life is over, I'll fly away." Passing wagons loaded with hay brought thoughts of freedom and the words, "Swing low, sweet chariot; coming for to carry me home." Work on the boat docks gave rise to "I stood on the banks of Jordan to see the ships come sailing over; oh, mourner, don't you weep when you see my ship sail by." Many of the songs had dual meanings, and when the masters thought that the slaves were merely enjoying themselves, in reality, they were making plans to escape from the plantation life before enjoying the peaceful life with the Lord in heaven. Sometimes when a slave was planning to run away, the others would begin to sing, "If you see my mother, tell her that you saw me, and when you saw me I was on my way. If you see my mother, tell her all about me; tell her that I'm coming home some day." Another song was, "One of these mornings bright and fair, I'm gonna take my wings and cleave the air. One of these morning, it won't be long; you'll look for me and I'll be gone."

When a slave finally made his escape, the master would discover that one was missing as he counted heads. The others would then sing, "Oh Satan's sad and I am glad; he done missed a soul he thought he had." Religion gave the promise of "a better day a'comin', hallelujah!" And they mustered the courage and patience to say, "Lord, I don't feel no ways tired."

The religious persuasion of the slaves was usually either Methodist or Baptist. Long before freedom came, the First Baptist Church was established in Williamsburg, Virginia, in 1776; in Richmond, Virginia, in 1780; in Savannah, Georgia, by Andrew Bryan in 1788. In 1813, the Union Church of Africa (Methodist) was established in Wilmington, Delaware. In 1816, the African Methodist Episcopal Church was established by Richard Allen. In 1821, the African Methodist Episcopal Zion Church was established by James Varick in New York City.

The year 1833 brought to fulfillment the prophecy of Revelation 6:13 foretelling that there would be seen in the heavens, myriads of shooting stars. Meteors showered the heavens from one end to another. It was an unforgettable sight to behold. The slaves came forth with a song "My Lord, what a morning when the stars began to fall!" John the Revelator had stated, "And the stars of heaven fell unto the earth, even as a fig tree casteth her untimely figs, when she is shaken by a mighty wind." Revelation 6:13.

The 1840s gave birth to the industrial revolution, a social revolution, and a religious revolution. New denominations sprang up, but most showed little interest in, or real concern for, the problems that slavery engendered and the need for the slaves to be set free. Some of these new groups were classed as "apologists."

This period saw the birth of the Church of Jesus Christ of Latter Day Saints, or Mormons, which had its beginnings in Illinois under Joseph Smith. It later moved to Utah under the leadership of Brigham Young. Their visions and teachings led them to believe that the Black person had no soul to save; however, the records will indicate that a Black sister was probably among the wives who went to Salt Lake City, Utah, with them when the church moved there.

The Christian Science Church was organized by Mary Baker Eddy in Boston, espousing the teachings that God is wholly good and powerful and that people are created by Him. No church dogma or penalty enforces reliance on prayer for healing, but it is a natural part of their way of life, healing being a state of the mind. The basic premise of Christian Science is that God is a divine Mind, the conceiver of man and the universe, and Mind is all that exists. Mind expresses itself in man. Spirit is eternal and real; matter is an unreal illusion subject to decay and dissolution. Evil has to do with matter; therefore, evil is unreal, an illusion. This was confusing to those who had been abused for hundreds of years, and few accepted this religion.

The modern spiritualist movement began in 1848 with Katherine and Margaret Fox, two little sisters from Hydesville, New York, near Rochester. The girls claimed that they had communicated with the spirit of a man who had been murdered in their house. The spirit supposedly answered their questions through a code of rapping sounds similar to the old voodoo practices in Africa.

The Disciples of Christ, headquartered at 221 Ohmer Avenue in Indianapolis, Indiana, developed in the United States during the early 1800s. Its full name is the Christian Church, and its founders included three men of Presbyterian background—Thomas Campbell and his son Alexander of Pennsylvania, along with Barton W. Stone of Kentucky. The church observes two ordinances—Communion, or the Lord's Supper, and Baptism— neither of which was administered to the slaves in those days. Many years passed before Blacks joined this church.

During this period, few if any Blacks were members of the Catholic Church, for it was experiencing difficulty holding on to its traditional membership. Protestantism was on the upswing, and Pope Gregory could not relate to the abolitionist movement that had erupted in America.

The Millerite group, which would later develop into the Seventh-day Adventist Church, had little if any regard for the slaves and did not share the gospel with them. A few Blacks did believe the biblical teachings of this group. In later years, an abundance of Blacks began to join as they began to labor for their own people.

There was a great religious awakening in the 1800s, giving rise to many of today's Christian organizations. However, most of them followed the line of the apologists and did not get involved in the abolition of the slave institution.

PIONEERS OF THE ADVENT MOVEMENT

William Miller

Josiah Litch

Joshua V. Himes

Joseph Bates

Charles Fitch

Chapter 10

The Rise Of Adventism In America
And The Disappointment

"And I took the little book out of the angel's hand, and ate it up, and it was in my mouth sweet as honey: and as soon as I had eaten it, my belly was bitter." Revelation 10:10

Seventh-day Adventism has its historical roots in New England in the teachings of William Miller, who began preaching in 1831, according to the *Review and Herald*, the denominational paper of the Seventh-day Adventist Church. Miller had been studying the books of Daniel and Revelation and was convinced from his study that Jesus was returning soon for His waiting church.

The movement was not confined to North America. Similar messages borne out of similar study of the Scriptures were heralded by various Bible students around the world—in England, Germany, Russia, France, Switzerland, Latin America, India, Africa, Asia and the Near East. However, it was in the United States under William Miller and William Foye that the proclamation reached its climax. They spoke of laying down the shackles of sin and of the joy of leaving this old world to go to live with God.

It should be noted that Black people were still suffering under the ravages of slavery. And it was during the summer of 1831 when all this religious fervor was growing that Nathan Turner led his revolt against White people in his quest for freedom for his people. Nathan Turner's preaching had also stirred the nation. Foye and Miller preached concerning the coming of the Lord and of the end of the world.

William Foye was one of the colored pioneers of the Advent Movement, who received visions relating to the coming of the Lord. Jerome Clark gives the following account in his book:

"In 1842 there lived in Boston an eloquent Baptist speaker preparing for the Episcopal ministry, William Foye. On January 18 and February 4 of that year he received two visions relating to the near advent of the Saviour, the journeying of the people of God to the heavenly city, the glories of the redeemed, and the joys of the new earth. He proclaimed what he had seen in a number of the churches, speaking to thousands in persuasive tones of the wonders of the heavenly world, the beauties of the New Jerusalem, and the pleasures of the saved. He continued this work until the fall of 1844, when he received a third vision which was not clear to him. In this vision he was shown a great platform, or step, on which large numbers of people stood. From time to time one of the group would drop through the platform out of sight. A voice said, 'apostatized,' after each such incident. He then saw the people rise to a second step, or platform, and noted that some dropped through that platform as well. At last a third platform appeared, extending to the very gates of the Holy City. A large company joined those who had advanced to this platform. Foye was unable to understand the vision he had received....

"Unaware that any message would be preached after October 22, Foye ceased his public speaking and did not proclaim the third message, or vision. Some time afterward in 1845, he heard Ellen Harmon relate the same vision he had refused to give. Shortly afterward he became sick and died. God had tried to use him, but he failed the trust, and another had taken his place."—*Religious Movements—1844*, Vol. 1, p. 72.

According to Jerome L. Clark, Hazen Foss received a vision similar to William Foye's, showing the people of God journeying to the City of God. "He was given several messages of warning to deliver and saw the trials and persecution that would come to him if he faithfully related what he had been shown. Like William Foye he saw three steps by which God's people were to approach the Holy City, but he was also perplexed by the idea of three steps, since he firmly believed that Christ was coming in a few more days. He shrank from the task and refused to relate the vision....

"Three months from the time of Hazen Foss's failure to relate his dream, he was in a home when he heard his vision being related by a young woman in an adjoining room. He was urged to come in to the meeting, but refused. As he heard the woman speak, the vision came back to him, and he realized that she was repeating it exactly as he had seen it. On seeing her afterward, he said, 'That is the instrument on whom the Lord has laid the burden.'

"That young woman was Ellen Gould Harmon,[11] who in 1844 was only seventeen years old. She was indeed the 'weakest of the weak'...."—*Religious Movement—1844*, Vol. 1, p. 74.

The Advent (Millerite) Movement led by William Miller and others reached its peak in 1843 and 1844 as the group prepared for the coming of Jesus. However, Miller and his followers did not think that the slaves would be in heaven, neither was the gospel to be taught to them. They adopted the popular position of the apologists, who believed that Blacks were not totally human and had no souls to save.

In addition, the Millerites were prejudiced against people who claimed to have had visions, and the fact that visions had come to William Foye and later to Hazen Foss, both people of color, did nothing to dispel the notion that

---

11   Ellen Gould (Harmon) White's oldest sister Mary was married to the brother of Hazen Foss, a man of mixed blood.

slaves were not likely candidates for heaven or to commend them as persons with whom the Advent message was to be shared.

Although most Blacks belonged to either the Methodist or Baptist Church and attended the services of one or the other on Sundays, a few did become participants in the Millerite Movement when it first began. Among those whose names are listed on the church rolls from the very beginning are two noted Black ministers—Charles Bowles, formerly a Free Will Baptist, and John W. Lewis of Providence, Rhode Island.

William Miller gave the same teachings about the coming of the Lord as the colored preacher William Foye, whom Dr. Delbert Baker in his book *The Unknown Prophet* calls the "John the Baptist" for Ellen G. (Harmon) White, the prophetess of the Seventh-day Adventist Church. Eunice Harmon carried her daughter Ellen to Foye's meetings at Beethoven Hall in Portland, Maine. Incidentally, Foye also attended one of Ellen G. White's meetings. According to Jacob Justiss, she had this to say about him, "…and I did know he was there; he is a great tall man…and he jumped right up…and praised the Lord. It was just what he had seen. I do not know what became of him."—*Angels in Ebony*, p. 15.

Christians of various religious persuasions were under conviction that the end of the world was at hand. Catholics, Baptists, Methodists, Quakers, Lutherans, Episcopalians were all of the same mind. When these people connected the end of the world with the coming of the Lord, slaves who heard the discussions while working in the houses and fields of the masters often would burst forth singing "Good news, the chariot's coming, and I don't want it to leave me behind."

The salvation that the Black person needed was embedded in the Advent Movement, but Black people were in slavery. This movement would bring freedom to the mind, the body and the soul, but Blacks were still in slavery. Regrettably, most Adventists were in sympathy with the slave owners, according to Ellen White in Volume 1 of *Testimonies for the Church*. They felt that they were ready for the judgment that would usher them into the kingdom of God, but they could not accept their Black brothers and sisters to make the journey along with them. They left their crops in the fields, reasoning that they would not have need for those earthly things in heaven. They were going to a land of milk and honey where they would never hunger or thirst again.

The slaves envisioning the judgment scene had sung, "You gotta stand the test in judgment; you got to stand it for yourself. There's nobody else can stand it for you; you gotta stand it by yourself." The institution of slavery delayed the Lord's return for the church in 1844. The apostle Paul had declared in the Epistle to the Hebrews, "that they, without us, would not be made whole."

History does not record the activities of Blacks in 1843 and 1844, the time when many supposed the end of the world would take place. Many slaves may have thought that the Lord was going to take them to heaven with the "saved." That would have meant an end to the rigors, trials, heartaches and griefs that they were experiencing under slavery. But the slaves, too, were eager for the Lord to come in 1844 as Miller, Foye and others had preached that He would. Could it be true? October 22, 1844, was a day of eager anticipation for the slaves also. They too watched, waited and prayed.

Miller was certain of his interpretation of the books of Daniel and Revelation concerning the 2300-day (year) prophecy. Something would happen in heaven. Jesus would come from glory for His people. They waited patiently but were embarrassed to find themselves still on earth when dawn came. Among the Adventist hopefuls were Captain Joseph Bates, Joshua V. Himes, Josiah Litch, Sylvester Bliss, Edward Stockman, George Storrs and Isaac Welcome. They were bitterly disappointed. The anticipation had been sweet, but reality brought sadness (Revelation 10:10). They slowly returned to their farms.

The slaves were also disappointed because they were still suffering under the slave system and would be for the next 19 years. They would continue to be oppressed and enslaved mentally, physically and spiritually, but they never gave up hope. The slaves never gave up the struggle but took courage and then exuberantly sang "Lord, I don't feel no ways tired, but I hope to shout glory when this world is on fire" or "There's a better day a'comin' when I'll leave this world of sorrow and join that holy number. Oh, glory, hallelujah."

The aftermath of the great disappointment produced varied reactions. When believers later came together in 1845, the majority of the Millerite Adventist leaders repudiated the movement and began a process of setting new dates, while some went into forms of religious fanaticism. But there was a minority who retained the faith that God had led in the Advent Movement teachings. The little band of believers held to the promise that He would come, and they resolved to watch and be ready.

One of the noteworthy members of the early Adventist group was a sea captain named Joseph Bates. Bates converted to Christianity during the 1820s and joined the Fairhaven Christian Church, along with his wife. He later accepted William Miller's views on the second advent and devoted his to the Millerite Movement. Being very sincere about his service to God, he finally accepted the beliefs espoused by James and Ellen White and became one of the founders of the Seventh-day Adventist Church. Joseph Bates took the Sabbath truths to the group after listening to Rachel (Oaks) Preston, a Seventh-day Baptist believer, who implored him to acknowledge the Creator of the universe by keeping Saturday as the day of worship according to the commandments.

By 1848, the wounds of bitterness caused by the disappointment had begun to heal, and the first general meeting of Sabbath-keeping Adventists was held in Rocky Hill, Connecticut. In 1849, the gospel tract Present Truth was published by their leader James E. White. He had been instructed to do this by his wife Ellen G. White, the prophetess, who said, "The Lord has shown me that you should begin a paper which will be little at first, but will grow." This was the beginning of the publishing work for the church, but it was against the law for Blacks to learn or to be taught how to read and write. By 1850 the second *Advent Review and Sabbath Herald* was published in Paris, Maine. It was still against the law for slaves to learn or to be taught to read and write.

While Miller was teaching about the end of the world and the coming of Jesus, Henry Highland Garnett, a Methodist minister, born a slave in Kent County, New Market, Maryland, became known for his anti-slavery sermons, another issue that was on everyone's lips at this time. Capitalizing on the popular Christian teachings, Garnett called for slaves to "strike for their lives and liberties," urging that the system of bondage made it impossible for them to obey the biblical commands to keep the Sabbath (as slaves, they were compelled to work on the Sabbath), to search the Scriptures (it was against the laws of the land for slaves to learn to read), to rear their children with respect for God's law (immorality was forced upon the slaves), and to worship only God (they were forced to obey their masters who sought to take the place of God and control the lives of the slaves).

Thus it was that in 1844, the Advent Movement was established in anticipation of the soon coming of the Lord but suffered a bitter disappointment because the members did not share the biblical truths with African-Americans who were still suffering under the rigors of slavery. The little band of believers held to the promise that He will come. "We will watch and be ready," they pledged. The Seventh-day Adventist Church, an outgrowth of that movement, holds that one day the everlasting gospel will be preached to every nation, kindred, tongue and people, and the joys of the hopeful will be fulfilled.

Chapter 11

Restlessness Changes The Nation's Attitudes

"...Thus saith the Lord, Let my people go, that they may serve me."
Exodus 8:1

Just as civil disobedience among African-Americans and other minorities brought speedy changes in the laws in America during the 1960s and 1970s, similar restlessness was seen across the land one hundred years earlier, during the 1840s.

People often find it difficult to make changes, especially when the call for change goes against established practices. Usually, a crisis must take place, tragedy must be experienced, an unbelievable problem must arise, death must strike, one's cherished possessions must be lost, something catastrophic must occur, or one must experience a genuine conversion to Jesus Christ to bring one to the knees to accept change.

A number of events transpired during the restless years of the early 19th century that brought about significant social, religious and political changes among the races and in the hearts of people around the world. One would never have dreamed that by the end of the century, the slaves would be free and would begin to share in the decision-making processes of government. It was inconceivable that former slave masters and former slaves would one day fellowship on the same level. But the stir of liberty was being felt everywhere among slaves. The strength of this new idea was too strong to pass by and continue business as usual. The embers of life, liberty and the pursuit of happiness would soon be fanned into a roaring flame that would never be put out. Both Whites and Blacks worked to bring about change. It took a civil war and the sacrifice of many lives, but lasting changes did take place.

Abuses endured by the slaves were never acceptable to this people, even though they were often beaten into submission. The dream of liberation was ever in their minds and was passed on from generation to generation. They constantly talked, sang, prayed and schemed in sundry ways and in diverse manners about how they could work with the Lord to achieve this goal for themselves and for their families.

Restlessness continued to stir the nation, and many stouthearted people, Black and White, initiated a program called the Underground Railroad to set captives free. This was an organized beginning to help slaves gain freedom, regardless of the price they had to pay. With this determination, many could often be heard singing about freedom. They sang "Freedom, oh freedom, freedom over me; and before I'll be a slave I'll be buried in my grave and go home to my Lord and be free" or "Steal away, steal away, steal away to Jesus."

Abraham Lincoln was elected to the presidency of the United States of America in 1860 and took office in January 1861. He had campaigned on a platform that dealt with unified preservation of the nation. He insisted that this nation could not stand if half of its people were slaves and half were free. This half slave and half free issue had also led to divisions among the churches in the North and the South over the morality of slavery.

In 1861, the American Civil War between the North and South was fought over the slave issue. At that time there were still 3,954 African slaves living in America. Many of them fought in the war to secure freedom for themselves and for their people. A number became insurgents, and some were runaways who had yoked up with the Indians in the hinterlands and swamps to spark terror in the hearts of the settlers, frontiersmen and, especially, slave owners.

Following the war, race relations across the South were very strained. In 1866, the year that my father Joseph Dudley was born in Dickson, Tennessee, race riots broke out in New Orleans, Louisiana, and in Memphis, Tennessee. Ex-slave soldiers who had fought in the war were abused, mistreated and lynched by the police who were deputized to uphold the law. An incident took place in Memphis in the Black neighborhood at Mississippi Boulevard and Walker Avenue, just one block from where a colored Seventh-day Adventist church would be located a few decades later. Two soldiers were killed and dragged through the streets behind a police car. This lynching marked the beginning of the race riot. Many White people found it difficult to accept the changes that were taking place. Similar events took place in New Orleans, Louisiana, where another riot broke out.

Although it cost him his life, President Lincoln courageously signed into law the Emancipation Proclamation, bringing an end to the institution of slavery. My grandfather Robert Talley was 47 years old and Grandmother Martha was 19 when freedom came. They lived in Hickman, Kentucky, not far from Paducah. With the signing of the proclamation, four of my uncles who were born slaves were also freed. Uncle Nathan stated that when the announcement was made in their community on August 8, 1863, they danced all night in the streets; they cried and sang "Free at last, free at last! Thank God, Almighty, we'se free at last!" Changes in the lifestyles of Black, the nation and the entire world were rapidly taking place, and conditions were never to be the same again.

However, change was hard to accept. Tensions were mounting everywhere. They needed to be quelled, and federal interventions were put in place throughout the South. When this took place, Blacks began to be elected to government posts and to assume other responsibilities for the first time in the history of the country. This brought on resentment from many White communities in the South.

When the Seventh-day Adventist denomination was officially organized in 1863, there were 3,500 members in the entire world. James White was selected as president, but he declined the post. John Byington then became the first president of the General Conference of Seventh-day Adventists.

In the wake of the Emancipation Proclamation, Blacks were no longer welcomed in the worship services of White congregations, and separate houses of worship for colored people were built. Winds of change were evident. Some few Blacks had become believers and members of the Seventh-day Adventist faith, but they were not permitted to attend the worship services in many places. It was difficult for many of these people who were heaven-bound soldiers in 1844 to accept the change.

"Byington's presidency not only had to deal with the problems of organizing the new church, but also the difficulties imposed by the Civil War. Adventism was confined to the Northern states and all were agreed that slavery had to end. Byington himself is said to have operated an Underground Railroad station on his Buck's Bridge farm."—*Adventist Heritage Magazine*, Spring, 1985, Vol. 10, No. 1, p. 48.

Among those who were sympathetic to the plight of freed Blacks and who worked toward better understanding among the races was John Harvey Kellogg who was born on February 26, 1862, in Battle Creek, Michigan, and later became the founder of the renown Kellogg Breakfast Cereal Corporation. His parents John P. and Ann (Stanley) Kellogg were members of the Underground Railroad system and took part in the abolitionist movement. John and Ann taught their children to love and respect all mankind. John Harvey developed the same convictions and upheld the same principles as his parents and performed many humanitarian deeds to help colored people. His actions, along with those of Ellen White, brought about changes in the way Seventh-day Adventist members related to these former slaves.

While on a trip to Florida, Kellogg spoke with Pastor John Frank Bookhart, Sr., a Black man, and told him that Bookhart's skin was more durable than that of White people because it stayed in tact longer. He punctured his own skin and that of Pastor Bookhart and rubbed the two arms together. "Now we are brothers by the mixing of blood," he said.

Many of Kellogg's views on the race issue were not shared by his White brothers and sisters. At one time, he brought 200 aborigines from Australia to Battle Creek for a visit. This greatly disturbed the people. He opened the doors of the Battle Creek School to all races and trained them to work for people around the world. He brought 30 Black children to his orphans' home in Battle Creek and placed elderly Blacks in his home for senior citizens. He opened settlement houses in the ghettos of Chicago, in the state of Florida, in other parts of the country and around the world. Kellogg wholeheartedly embraced the changes that were taking place in the nation. Regrettably, before he passed away in 1943, the leaders of the Seventh-day Adventist Church had disfellowshipped him from the church. He never joined another church. He was among many who sacrificed greatly to bring about changes within and outside of the church.

Also in 1866, the American Missionary Societies from the North began setting up schools for the children of former slaves. In Nashville, Tennessee, Fisk University was established. Lemoyne College was established in Memphis; Tugaloo College in Jackson, Mississippi; Knoxville College in Tennessee; Hampton Institute in Hampton, Virginia; and Howard University in Washington, D.C. The Adventists finally joined the movement to help educate the former slaves by opening the Huntsville Training School in Huntsville, Alabama, in 1896. Blacks were not allowed to attend schools established for White children. Many Whites found it difficult to accept change.

The Catholic Church accepted the changes brought about when liberty came to the slaves in America and began instituting programs to help Blacks get settled in their new roles and to make converts of them. The church had done similar works in other parts of the world. These determined Blacks had endured hardship and privation as good Christian soldiers and, in time, would prove to be a strong influence for the church among many nations of the world. Black influence, in time, would have a bearing on race relations throughout the world, and the church needed to be ready for it.

With each passing decade, new generations came to realize and accept the changes that were taking place. No force is stronger than an idea whose time has come. An end to slavery in 1863 was an idea whose time had come, and it brought about changes in individual attitudes, in the governments of the world, in society, in religion, and in the concept of brotherhood.

Chapter 12

The Civil War, The Church And The Slave Institution

A division in the Methodist and Baptist churches in America over the slave issue helped to spark the Civil War, causing much bloodshed. Many of these church members were also members of the United States Congress, and their agitation finally led to the outbreak of the Civil War and the signing of the Emancipation Proclamation by President Abraham Lincoln.

Othal Hawthorne Lakey gives this account of what took place: "Because of a schism in American Methodism, divisions began to arise in the church, not because of doctrinal differences, but because of various conceptual differences. There came into being the Republican Methodists, the Christian Church (Disciples of Christ) and the Methodist Protestant Church.

"The roots of the great division over slavery go back to the conference of 1784, which outlawed slavery in slave states; however, it soon became necessary to modify the anti-slavery position of the church. In religious circles two groups concerning slavery could be found: (1) the apologists; and (2) the abolitionists. The Abolitionist Movement in the North found numerous adherents among New England and New York Methodists. In the Methodist General Conferences of 1836 and 1840 the moderates of the North combining with the Southern delegates out-voted the abolitionists by a large majority and imposed a 'gag rule' on the church, prohibiting the discussion of slavery in all Methodist conferences. This action led to a withdrawal of the most extreme abolitionists wing under the leadership of Orange Scott (1800–1847), LeRoy Sunderland (1802–1885) and L. Matlock (1816–1884), and the formation of the Wesleyan Methodist Church (Connection) of America in 1843. This session brought about a shift among the moderates of the North when they saw that in their attempt to avoid a pro-slavery secession they had precipitated an anti-slavery division.

"The most serious division over slavery came as a result of the action taken by the Methodist General Conference of 1844. (This is the year that the Adventist believers under the leadership of William Miller, the mulatto preacher William Foye, Joseph Bates, Joshua V. Himes, Josiah Litch and others anticipated that the kingdom of heaven would literally come to earth the world would come to an end and the people of God would be taken to heaven and be freed from the troubles of the world.) The issue among the Methodist was brought to a head when one of its bishops, James O. Andrews, became married to a 'slave-holding' wife under the state laws of Georgia prohibiting manumission (liberation or the emancipation of a slave). After eleven days of debate a motion to suspend Bishop Andrews was passed by a substantial majority. A few days later a plan of separation was adopted by an almost unanimous vote. In Louisville, Kentucky in May of 1845, the Methodist Episcopal Church, South, was organized. Its General Conference met in Petersburg, Virginia in May of 1846. The doctrine, polity and discipline of the southern church were identical with those of the Methodist Episcopal Church, even retaining the same rule on slavery. The southern church began with a membership of 460,000, of whom 124,906 were Blacks and 2,972 were Indians.

"A small schism was that of Free Methodists, who broke from the General Conference about 1850 charging that American Methodists had departed from the true Wesleyan heritage."—*History of the Colored Methodist Episcopal Church*, pp. 101–129.

While in vision, Ellen G. White saw the war developing and prophesied:

"January 4, 1862, I was shown some things in regard to our nation. My attention was called to the Southern rebellion. The South had prepared themselves for a fierce conflict, while the North were asleep as to their true feelings. Before President Lincoln's administration commenced, great advantage was taken by the South. The former administration (James Buchanan 1857–1861) planned and managed for the South to rob the North of their implements of war. They had two objectives for so doing: 1. They were contemplating a determined rebellion and must prepare for it; 2. When they should rebel, the North would be wholly unprepared. They would thus gain time, and by their violent threats and ruthless course they thought they could intimidate the North that they would be obliged to yield to them and let them have everything their own way.... The North had no just idea of the strength of the accursed system of slavery. It is this and this alone, which lies at the foundation of the war.

"As the war was shown to me, it looked like the most singular and uncertain that has ever occurred. A great share of volunteers enlisted fully believing that the result of the war would be to abolish slavery. Others enlisted intending to be very careful to keep slavery just as it is, but to put down rebellion and preserve the Union. And then to make the matter still more perplexing and uncertain, some of the officers in command are strong proslavery men whose sympathies are all with the South, yet who are opposed to a separate government.... Some of our leading men in Congress also are constantly working to favor the South. In this state of things, proclamations are issued for national fasts, for prayer that God will bring this war to a speedy and favorable termination....

"I saw that these national fasts were an insult to Jehovah. He accepts of no such fasts. The recording angel writes in regard to them: 'Ye fast for strife and debate, and to smite with the fist of wickedness.' I was shown how our leading men have treated the poor slaves who have come to them for protection. Angels have recorded it. Instead of breaking their yoke and letting the oppressed go free, these men have made the yoke more galling for them than when in the service of their tyrannical masters. Love of liberty leads the poor slaves to leave their masters and risk their lives to obtain liberty. They would never venture to leave their masters and expose themselves to the difficulties and horrors attending their recapture if they had not as strong a love for liberty as any of us."—*Testimonies for the Church*, Vol. 1, pp. 253–254, 256–257.

When the war finally broke and thousands of lives were sacrificed, Ellen White prophesied:

"God is punishing this nation for the high crime of slavery. He has the destiny of the nation in His hands. He will punish the South for the sin of slavery and the North for so long suffering its overreaching and overbearing influence.

"The system of slavery has reduced and degraded human beings to the level of the brutes, and the majority of slave masters regard them as such. The consciences of these masters have become seared and hardened, as was Pharaoh's and if compelled to release their slaves, their principles remain unchanged, and they would make the slaves feel their oppressive power if possible."—*Ibid*, pp. 264, 265.

It was during this period, with social, religious and industrial challenges taking place across the nation, that the Seventh-day Adventist denomination was coming into being. The church was not a recognized organized body until 1863, but before this, the work of evangelizing and building up the membership had begun. Very few Blacks accepted the teachings of this new-found faith, however.

J. N. Loughborough, M. E. Olsen, Ellen G. White and F. N. Wilcox, spokespersons for the church, stated in one of the denomination's church history books that the problems of the little struggling, but growing Seventh-day Adventist Church were many during the perplexing days of the Civil War period. It was not troubled with a great sectional cleavage of the North and the South. Other large Protestant denominational churches floundered and split into two antagonistic and conflicting groups. Providence spared this church from this catastrophe, because it had not yet expanded into the South; however, as has been noted in the writings of Ellen White, some of the members of the church sympathized with the slaveholders, and even to this day, similar attitudes can be found within the hearts of some.

Regarding this attitude, Mrs. White wrote: "There are a few in the ranks of the Sabbath keepers who sympathize with the slaveholder. When they embraced the truth, they did not leave behind them all the errors they should have left. They need a more thorough draft from the cleansing fountain of truth…. They maintain that the slave is the property of the master, and should not be taken from him. They rank these slaves as cattle and say that it is wronging the owner just as much to deprive him of his slaves as to take away his cattle. I was shown that it mattered not how much the master had paid for human flesh and the souls of men; God gives him no title to human souls, and he has no right to hold them as his property. Christ died for the whole human family, whether White or Black. The institution of slavery does away with this and permits man to exercise over his fellow man a power which God has never granted him, and which belongs alone to God. The slave master has dared assume the responsibility of God over his slave, and accordingly he will be accountable for the sins, ignorance, and vice of the slave. He will be called to an account for the power which he exercises over the slave. The colored race are God's property. Their Maker alone is their master, and those who have dared chain down the body and the soul of the slave, to keep him in degradation like the brutes, will have their retribution. The wrath of God has slumbered, but it will awake and be poured out without mixture of mercy."—*Ibid*, p. 358.

Some of the founders of the church, however, had been members of the Methodist denomination and were abolitionists. Many were a part of the Underground Railroad resistance group which helped many slaves to freedom. Ellen G. White constantly kept before the members that there should be a disregard for the Fugitive Slave Laws that had been passed to return runaway slaves to their masters. She encouraged civil disobedience. She wrote:

"The law of our land requiring us to deliver a slave to his master, we are not to obey; and we must abide the consequences of violating this law. The slave is not the property of any man. God is his master, and man has no right to take God's workmanship into his hands and claim him as his property."—*Ibid*, p. 202.

Many bemoan the number of troops that died in the Civil War. Not only did White men die during this conflict, but thousands of Black troops died to set their people free and to preserve the union. The troops were segregated, but they fought valiantly.

In the first weeks after the fall of Fort Sumpter, northern Blacks joined in the outburst of patriotism and offered their services to the government to help suppress the rebellion that had begun from the leaders in the South. The government and the northern people considered it a White man's war and refused to accept the offers. Nevertheless, Black leaders continued to urge the necessity of enrolling Black troops. They knew that if Blacks were given the opportunity to prove their patriotism and courage on the field of battle, the nation would be morally obligated to grant them first class citizenship. As Frederick Douglass put it, "Once let the Black man get upon his person the brass letters, U.S., let him get an eagle on his button, a musket on his shoulder and bullets in his pocket, and there is no power on earth which can deny that he has earned the right to citizenship in the United States.

"Douglass was one of the most persistent and eloquent advocates of arming the Negro. In August, 1861, when the war was more than four months old and the North had yet to win a major victory, Douglass chided the government in an editorial entitled 'Fight Rebels with Only One Hand.'

"In January 1863 the War Department authorized Governor John Andrew of Massachusetts to raise a regiment of Negro soldiers in his state. Massachusetts called upon the wealthy abolitionist George L. Stearns to form a committee of 'prominent citizens' to raise money for the recruitment of men for the Fifty-fourth Massachusetts Regiment from all over the North. Stearns hired several Negro leaders as recruiting agents, including Frederick Douglass, William Wells Brown, Charles L. Remond, John Mercer Langston, Henry Highland Garnett, and Martin R. Delany. These men traveled all through the North and even into Canada, urging Black men to join the army.

"On May 1, 1863, the *New York Tribune* observed that most Northerners now approved of the policy of arming Negroes, but that many still doubted whether they would make good soldiers. On May 27, 1863, two regiments of New Orleans free Negroes and Louisiana ex-slaves participated in an assault on Port Hudson, a Confederate stronghold on the lower Mississippi.... The Black forces consisted of the First Louisiana, under Lieutenant Col. Basset and the Third Louisiana, under Col. Nelson.... One of the most efficient of officers was Capt. Andre Calix, a man whose identity with his race could not be mistaken; for he prided himself of being the blackest man in the Crescent City.... This regiment petitioned their commander to allow them to occupy the post of danger in the battle, and it was granted.... Their assault was awesome. A White officer of engineers who witnessed the assault declared that 'you have no idea how my prejudice with regard to Negro troops have been dispelled by the battle the other day. The brigade of Negroes behaved magnificently and fought splendidly; could not have done better. They are far superior in discipline to the White troops, and just as brave.'

"Fully convinced of the utility of a large Negro army, the union government extended its recruiting activities to the border slave states in 1863–64. Although the brutality of impressment characterized the operations of some recruiters in these area as it had elsewhere, most of the freedmen who joined the army in the border states did so voluntarily. The Negroes in Nashville held a meeting on October 20, 1863 where a Black leader declared: 'Then let every able bodied descendant of Africa rally to arms, for arms alone will achieve our rights. God will rule over our destinies. He will guide us, for He is the friend of the oppressed and down-trodden. The God of battles will watch over us and lead us. We have nothing to lose, but everything to gain. Then why not enter upon the work with holy zeal, and throw ourselves with might and main into the breach? The decision of the great questions of the day rest with us.... Slavery can never be what it has been, but let us not sit supinely, but rather take a share in the great events transpiring. Let us make a name for ourselves

The Black Soldier

and race, bright as the noonday sun. Let us show, as Greece has done, a people bursting their bonds and rallying for freedom.... Present to the world a picture of manhood; show yourselves lion-hearted; be not afraid to die.' "—*The Negro's Civil War*, pp. 187–196.

In assault after assault the Black soldiers engaged the enemy and the Lord blessed them to prevail in these battles. In fact, Ellen G.White, the prophetess stated that the angels fought by their sides.

At the battle at Manassas, Virginia, at the beginning of the war, the Northern soldiers were about to be massacred. Ellen G. White describes what happened in the following manner: "...an angel descended and waved his hand backward. Instantly there was confusion in the ranks. It appeared to the Northern men that their troops were retreating, when it was not so in reality, and a precipitated retreat commenced.... And had the Northern army at this time pushed the battle still further in their fainting, exhausted condition, the far greater struggle and destruction which awaited them would have caused great triumph in the South. God would not permit this, and sent an angel to interfere. The sudden falling back of the Northern troops is a mystery to all. They know not that God's hand was in the matter.

The Black Soldier in the Civil War

"The destruction of the Southern army was so great that they had no heart to boast. The sight of the dead, the dying and the wounded gave them but little courage to triumph. This destruction, occurring when they had advantage, and the North great disadvantage, caused them much perplexity."—*Testimonies for the Church Vol. I*, pp. 266, 267.

Although they did not participate in the battles with the troops, there were women who played leading roles in championing the rights of the slaves. Isabella Baumforce, better known as Sojourner Truth, was one who helped to spark the Abolitionist Movement and the Underground Railroad. She kept the cause for freedom agitated. In later years she became a member of the Seventh-day Adventist denomination.

Another woman who played a major role during and before the war was Harriet Tubman who served as a spy for the Northern army. Once she accepted a ride offered by one of the servants of the big house. As they rode along, he noticed the paper coat that she wore and questioned what it was. She replied that it was just her petticoat with which she was trying to keep warm. He never knew that the papers were documents telling of various Southern troop movements.

Julia Ward Howe in her song "The Battle Hymn of the Republic," spoke of angels who fought on the side of freedom: "I have seen Him in the watch fires of a hundred circling camps; they have builded him an altar in the evening dews and damps. I can read his righteous sentence by the dim and flaring lamps; His truth is marching on."

When the war ended, the enslaved realized that the Lord had answered their prayers and delivered them from the lion's den just as He had delivered Daniel.

In 1884, the prophetess in looking down through the stream of time prophesied that slavery will return for Sabbath-keeping people. She stated:

"As the defenders of truth refuse to honor the Sunday-sabbath, some of them will be thrust into prison, some will be exiled, some will be treated as slaves. To human wisdom all this now seems impossible; but as the restraining Spirit of God shall be withdrawn from men, and they shall be under the control of Satan, who hates the divine precepts, there will be strange developments. The hearts can be very cruel when God's fear and love are removed.

"But many of all nations and all classes, high and low, rich and poor, black and white will be cast into the most unjust and cruel bondage. The beloved of God pass weary days, bound in chains, shut in by prison bars, sentenced to be slain, some apparently left to die of starvation in dark loathsome dungeons. No human ear is open to hear their moans, no human hand is ready to lend them help.

"Will the Lord forget His people in this trying hour? Did He forget faithful Noah when judgments were visited upon the antediluvian world? Did He forget Lot when the fire came down from heaven to consume the cities of the plain? Did He forget Elijah when the oath of Jezebel threatened him with the fate of the prophets of Baal? Did He forget Jeremiah in the dark and dismal pit of his prison house? Did He forget the three worthies in the fiery furnace or Daniel in the den of lions?

" 'Zion said, The Lord hath forsaken me, and my Lord hath forgotten me. Can a woman forget her suckling child, that she should not have compassion on the son of her womb? Yea, they may forget, yet will I not forget thee.

Behold, I have graven thee upon the palms of My hands.' Isaiah 49:14–16. The Lord of hosts has said: 'He that toucheth you toucheth the apple of His eye.' Zechariah 2:8."—*The Great Controversy*, pp. 608, 626.

"...our country shall repudiate every principle of its Constitution as a Protestant and republican government."—*Testimonies for the Church*, Vol. 5, p. 451.

During World War II, Japanese-Americans were placed in concentration camps, although most of them were American born. Adolph Hitler placed millions of Jewish people in concentration camps and put six million to death in ovens during the same time. When civil disobedience flared in America during the 1960s and 70s, concentration camps were being prepared to incarcerate the dissidents. Nelson Mandela, the prime minister of South Africa spent 27 years in prison in that land because he dared to hold to the principle of fairness and freedom. Today, God's Spirit is being withdrawn from the earth and Satan's forces are loose in the earth. God commissions: "Sound the message, every captive may be free."

Chapter 13

Religions Of African-Americans After The Emancipation

A number of churches had been established in the New World following the Protestant Reformation. There was the Methodist Church in a number of segments (Republican, Canadian, American, Methodist Episcopal, North and South, Free Methodists, African Methodist Episcopal, Congregational, African Methodist Episcopal Zion, and Episcopal), as well as Disciples of Christ, the American and Southern Baptists, the Quakers, Christian Science, the Spiritualists, the Latter Day Saints, the Seventh-day Adventists and the Catholics. After being emancipated, these freed men and women were left to make decisions regarding which religious body they would affiliate with, if any. It appeared that the majority of them had Methodist and Baptist inclinations. Many joined no church at all.

The Methodist and Baptist churches in America had split over the slave issue. There were Northern and Southern organizations in both denominations, although the policy was much the same; however, the Methodist had what was known as the "Central Jurisdiction," while the individual Baptist congregation was an entity unto itself. These denominations had strong influences before the war. The African Methodist Episcopal and the African Methodist Episcopal Zion organizations had also been established before the war; the A. M. E. was established in 1787, and the A. M. E. Zion in 1796. After the war, both organizations sought to woo the freed men and women to join them.

The African Methodist Episcopal Church was organized in Philadelphia, Pennsylvania, in 1787 by Bishop Richard Allen and Pastor Absalom Jones because they were continually being harassed when they sought to worship at the established church. The following incident as related by James E. Hurt in his *National Assembly of Black Church Organizations,* explains what finally drove these men to establish this new church for Blacks:

"In the year 1786, Allen while preaching at St. George's Church, envisioned a vast opportunity in seeking out and instructing his African brethren, who were a forgotten and neglected people. He would gather for prayer meeting and was known to conduct four or five sermons a day.

"When large numbers of these religiously inspired Blacks began to attend St. George's Church, they were removed from their original seats and placed around the wall. On other occasions, they were sent to the gallery. Dissatisfaction with such arrangements steadily increased. One Sunday morning, a group of the trustees at St. George's Church attempted to pull Rev. Absalom Jones up off his knees while in prayer. After making the statement 'we will go

FOUNDERS OF FIRST COLORED DENOMINATIONS

*Moses C. Clayton—First
Colored Baptist Church in
Baltimore Maryland—1836*

*Richard Allen—A. M. E.
Church—1787*

James Varick—A. M. E. Zion Church—1796

Mother Liberty C. M. E. Church

Mother Liberty C. M. E. Church—Jackson, Tennessee

William Miles,
first C. M. E. Church Bishop

out, never to trouble you no more,' Allen and his friends walked out of the church in a body, never to return. Because of this unkind treatment and the other restrictions placed upon the worshipers of African descent, in 1787, pastors Richard Allen and Absalom Jones withdrew from St. George's Methodist."—*National Assembly of Black Church Organizations*, p. 118.

Thus, in 1787 the African Methodist Episcopal Church was organized in the city of Philadelphia, Pennsylvania, and spread to many places around the world where people of color were found.

Before the revolt of Haitian slaves in 1791, the New York Society for Promoting the Manumission of Slaves was founded in 1785. This organization and unfavorable events between the races created a new assertiveness among Blacks, and a new movement in Methodism created a groundswell for freedom and self-expression.

"October 1796 saw the culmination of dreams and hard work by Blacks, as the African Methodist Episcopal Zion Church was founded in New York City.

"A group of Blacks, led by James Varick and others, withdrew from John Street Methodist Church. They held meetings in a house near 'The Collect Pond' on Cross Street between Orange and Mulberry from 1796 to 1800. Most of the church leaders were free, but a large number of the members were still slaves...The first annual conference held in 1821 was attended by nineteen preachers, representing six churches. In 1822, the year when the children of slaves were returned to their African continent (and Liberia), James Varick was made the first Bishop of the A. M. E. Zion Church. It was part of the Zionist Movement of 1822—*Ibid*, p. 121.

"The American Baptist Home Missionary Society was organized in New York City on April 27, 1832, for the purpose of (1) establishing churches and Sunday Schools and giving the gospel to the destitute, (2) aiding in the erection of church edifices, and (3) providing normal and theological schools for the freedmen and Indians.

"Between 1839 and 1869 every major religious body in America strained with tension. In 1844, the Foreign Mission Board refused to recommend a Georgian slaveholder for appointment as missionary to the Cherokee Indians. This resulted in a growing chasm between the friends and foes of slavery. The inevitable separation of Northern and Southern Baptists was the result.

"After the 1845 separation, Baptists in the South continued special religious and moral instruction among Negroes, and in many instances both shared the same building and the same services.

"Negroes were not really accepted by...Whites, especially the free Negroes, and laws forbidding assemblies were strictly enforced. Reverend R. B. C. Howell was the main force in encouraging the withdrawal from the White church. In fact he was one of the first ministers to insist upon separate services for the Negroes.

"Heretofore, Negroes had worshiped every Sunday afternoon on the lower floor of the church building with all the advantages of a separate organization.

"About 1845, the Old City School House was obtained and Samuel A. Davidson of Lynchburg, Virginia, was ordained and placed in charge of the group. The Negro membership expanded until the White membership thought it best to build them a house 'of worship' in 1849."

"The Blacks in the Baptist Church instituted what became known as the National Baptist Convention. These established the Roger Williams College in Nashville, Tennessee, which later became the American Baptist Theology Seminary."—*Ventures In Education With Black Baptists in Tennessee*, pp. 11.

These and similar situations marked the beginnings of the Black Baptist Church in America. The Baptists congregations today consists of Progressive Baptists, National Baptists, Hardshell and Missionary Baptists.

We turn again to the Methodists and the organization of the Colored Methodist Episcopal Church in 1870. There were thousands of former slaves who previously had attended the churches of their former masters in the South. The Methodists decided to organize the General Conference of the Colored Methodist Episcopal Church, which took place in Jackson, Tennessee, on December 16, 1870. The Methodists had already established seven "colored conferences" before the war began. The organization of the new denomination was already in place. The first two colored bishops were William H. Miles, a mulatto from Kentucky, and Richard H. Vanderhorst, a Black man from South Carolina. The church, it seems, was literally the "colored" church with roots reaching back to the Negro and colored debates of 1831 and 1855 when a third race of people was officially documented by the legislature for the state of Delaware. A Negro could be colored but a colored was not a Negro, thus there came into being the Colored Methodist Episcopal Church. During the earlier days, it seems as if only people of a certain skin pigmentation could belong. As successive generations were born, the practice tended to change; however, there are still some who desire to be identified as "Colored." Bishop Othal Hawthorne Lakey in his book entitled *The History of the CME Church* states:

"By 1870, the social and political climate of the Reconstruction period, along with the demonstrated ability of colored leaders within the church to conduct their own affairs, indicated that the time had come to transplant the new growing plant of a colored church from the ecclesiastical greenhouse of the M. E. Church, to the soil of Black independence and control...Pursuant to the call by the bishops of the M. E. Church, South for a General Conference for colored members of the five colored annual conferences that had been organized and reported to the General Conference—(1) Tennessee, (2) Kentucky, (3) Mississippi, (4) Alabama, and (5) Georgia...We remember that the General Conference had suggested that other colored conferences be organized before the Colored General Conference convened...Accordingly, what might be termed 'quasi-colored annual conferences'—i.e., conferences that had not been organized and were not functioning as separate colored conferences— were represented. Texas, Arkansas and South Carolina...Virginia."—*The History of the CME Church*, pp. 190, 191.

These people took a posture that they would not join the A. M. E. or the A. M. E. Zion organizations because they were considered to be offshoots of the original Methodist church whose roots extended to the Wesleys in England. They would not continue in the Methodist Episcopal, South, because that organization had kept them in slavery. Thus, they chose a separate organization and named it the Colored Methodist Episcopal Church. During the years of the Civil Rights Movement, there was a name change to Christian Methodist Episcopal Church in order to stay in touch with the times. In 1895, my grandparents joined with Pastor Warren Thomas and 16 other former slaves to establish our family church, Warren Chapel C. M. E. Church in Hickman, Kentucky.

One of the fastest growing denominations among Blacks in America is the Church of God in Christ. It originated in the Holiness Revival Movement of the middle 18th century. The denomination was established within the mainstream churches under the stewardship of an interdenominational body known as the National Holiness Association. The aim of this organization was to revive interest in John Wesley's doctrine of sanctification—an area of Methodism that was thought to have been neglected for some time.

Bishop Charles H. Mason founded the church in 1907 in Lexington, Mississippi, after he was dismissed from the Baptist Church for advocating baptism with the Holy Ghost and "fire" and the speaking in tongues.

A significant number of Negroes apparently were not comfortable with the Methodist and Baptist style of worship, which reflected the European "high mass" type of worship expression. They longed for something more closely akin to their African customs of worship, which they never completely surrendered under the dictates of the masters. Their worship included drums, dancing and singing that expressed their moods, feelings and experiences. They wanted a more "spirit-filled" service. This concern came to the attention of the Church of God in Christ leaders who responded to what they felt were the expressed needs of Negroes by establishing places where they could worship in their "own way."

From the first location in Lexington, Mississippi, this church established "store front" congregations for Negroes, especially as they moved North. Finally, they began to construct beautiful houses of worship that attracted many. This church is one of the fastest growing predominantly Black religious organizations in existence today, with a membership of over seven million members and 10,000 congregations.

Very few Blacks were members of the Catholic Church during the days of slavery. This church has been very supportive of Blacks since getting a foothold in America. Quite a change took place in the church after the rise of the abolitionist movement when Pope Gregory refused to become involved in the struggle and took a posture that he would not interfere in the slave question.

When the Seventh-day Adventist denomination finally took hold in the Black community, a fairly large number of its congregations met in "storefront" places of worship. Because of this, it was sometimes mistaken for the Church of God in Christ. Many of the members of the Black sector had religious and social backgrounds similar to those in the Colored Methodist Episcopal Church. The impression in the Black community was that only fair-skinned persons would be accepted into its membership. Interestingly enough, a number of these members boldly announced that they were not Negroes but colored people. The impression soon changed as people of all colors and hues began to announce that they were Seventh-day Adventist.

The church was organized the same year that the Civil War came to an end, in 1863. Although Blacks were a part of the original group in 1844, they were few in number. By 1887, there were less than ten Black members of the church, and the leaders had grave concerns about opening its doors to former slaves. At a General Conference session held in San Francisco, California, they tabled the issue when it was brought to the floor rather than discuss it. However, Blacks began to accept the teachings of the church and in 1900, there were 50 baptized members. We do not know whether or not their names were placed on the official church records at the time.

The numbers began to increase tremendously at the turn of the century when separate congregations were organized. Some of these congregations were larger than some conferences, which led to requests for the establishment of colored conferences as the Methodist denomination had done in 1870.

The Anglican Church, the Church of Christ, the Christian Science, the Church of the Latter Day Saints and others had small memberships and very few, if any, Black believers before or after the Civil War.

After the war and up until 1995, the membership of Blacks among the various denominations makes for an interesting insight into religion and race relations. In 1995, the religious populations in the Black communities in the United States were shown to be as follows: National Baptist Convention, USA—7.2 million; Church of God in Christ—5.0 million; National Baptist Convention of America—3.5 million; Progressive Baptist Convention—3.0 million; African Methodist Episcopal Zion—2.5 million; Catholic—2.0 million; Seventh-day Adventist—230,000.

The overall religious bodies number Evangelical Protestants as being 25.9% of the religious Community; 23.4% are Roman Catholic; 18.5%, Non-religious; 18.0%, Mainline Protestant; 7.8%, Black Protestants; 3.3%, Jewish; and 1.1% other religions; (Muslims—0.4%, Hindus—0.2%, Buddhists—0.2% and others—0.3%)—*Time Magazine*, 1995.

While the Seventh-day Adventist denomination was in its formative years, Ellen G. White began to lay strong emphasis on the duty that the church had to share the gospel with these former slaves. She chided the leaders concerning their "duty to the colored people."

Chapter 14

Our Duty To The Colored People

"I do not mean to live a coward or die a coward, leaving my work undone,
I must follow in my Master's footsteps...The Black man's name is written in
the book of life beside the White man's. All are one in Christ"
—The Southern Work, pp. 10, 11

"The Spirit of the Lord God is upon me because the Lord hath anointed me to preach good tidings unto the meek, he hath sent me to bind up the brokenhearted, to proclaim liberty to the captives, and the opening of the prison to them that are bound." Isaiah 61:1.

After the Emancipation proclamation was signed and Blacks were free, the roads were filled with former slaves drifting from place to place. The Civil War, just ended, had divided the nation into two camps. Brother was against brother. Attitudes developed; barriers were built; race discrimination escalated; riots broke out. But the commission of God was still before His people to share the message of His undying love and grace with every nation, kindred, tongue and people.

The future was filled with uncertainty for the people who had been held captive for over 400 years. They were somewhat uncertain about what to do and in which direction to turn. They had no place in particular to go—no place to call "home." Many wandered in search of loved ones separated by the slave institution. They were bewildered, frightened, angry; others were joyful and most grateful to God for bringing them deliverance.

Many gravitated toward the cities only to find conditions had changed; tempers between the races were rising. In 1866, three years after the proclamation, race riots broke out in New Orleans and Memphis and later in St. Louis, places where former slaves gathered in clusters.

They had been cared for by the masters for decades and centuries. Their food, shelter and clothing (such as they were) were provided by him; decisions about their welfare were all made by the master; now, they must fend, plan and work for themselves. It was a challenging but not an insurmountable task. Some had practically run the master's house back on the plantation. They had worked the fields, planted, harvested and carried the crops to market and laid food in store for the winter months and lean days that were to come. They had helped to build the mansions; their women had run the houses and reared the White children while the women of the house entertained her guests who came from far and near. Most possessed latent skills and leadership qualities. They were knowledgeable about many things. Now, entering this new chapter of their lives, they needed formal training in order to be successful in a cold and unfriendly world.

The need for centers of learning in the South was met by various groups, including the religious organizations and the local and national governments. Missionary societies moved South to help with reconstruction. The government changed the political climate to acquaint Blacks with the political system. Some became mayors, congressmen and even governors in some states. Educators established learning centers and schools throughout the South for the colored people and poor Whites. In these schools, people were trained to become teachers and preachers, to become responsible leaders.

In 1866 Fisk University and Central Tennessee College were founded in Nashville, Tennessee, for the training of colored youth. Members of the First Congregational Society proposed setting up a school for freed Blacks in Washington, D. C. The school was chartered and opened its doors in 1867; thus, government-supported Howard University was established and named for General Oliver Otis Howard, who headed the post-war Freedman's Bureau.

Roger Williams University (American Baptist Theological Seminary) opened its doors in 1867 in Nashville, Tennessee; Hampton Institute was founded in Hampton, Virginia, near Newport News in 1868; Lemoyne Institute began its long record of service in Memphis, Tennessee, in 1869; Knoxville College was founded by the Presbyterians in Knoxville, Tennessee, in 1871. Meharry Medical College was established by the Methodists during the 1870s. Lane College was established by Bishop Isaac Lane under the guidance of the newly independent Colored Methodist Church in Jackson, Tennessee, in 1879; they also established Collins Chapel Hospital in nearby Memphis. Tugaloo College was founded near Jackson, Mississippi. Mr. and Mrs. Theodore Troy, parents of Owen A. Troy, Sr., came from Wilberforce University in Oberlin, Ohio, to serve as instructors. Troy later was one of the colored leaders who helped to develop the Seventh-day Adventist church among his people.

All historically Black institutions of higher learning are located in the South, with the exception of Lincoln University in Pennsylvania and Wilberforce University in Ohio.

Tuskegee Institute was established by an act of the Alabama State Legislature in 1881. Booker T. Washington, a promising student at Hampton Institute in 1872, was invited to serve as its principal and instructor. He remained for 33 years. Under his administration, students flocked to the school from across the nation and around the world. Born to a slave, his aim was "to lift the veil of ignorance and superstition from the eyes of his people."

Booker T. became the political "colored magnet" of the nation under President Theodore Roosevelt during the Spanish-American War and during the days of "Roosevelt's Rough Riders." In colored circles, he was known as the "Wizard of Tuskegee." He developed a philosophy of training the hand.

OUR DUTY TO THE COLORED PEOPLE

Booker T. Washington

W. E. B. Dubois

Booker T. Washington with staff and student body at Tuskegee

Fisk Jubilee Singers of Nashville, Tennessee

With this concept he won the hearts of many Southern and Northern Whites who gave tremendous financial support to building the school.

Dr. George Washington Carver, a native of St. Joseph, Missouri, joined Booker T. Washington at Tuskegee and served as one of the institute's best-known instructors from 1896 until his death in 1943. God taught him many uses for the products of the soil such as the peanut and the sweet potato.

W. E. B. Dubois, one of the founding fathers of Fisk University espoused a different philosophy from that of Booker T. Washington. "Train the mind!" was his concept of helping students to meet the challenges in life. They had learned to use their hands to do many things, he chided. Now the mind must be developed. All brains are equal; the difference lies in how they are developed. "Train the mind!" Leaders must be trained to meet the challenges that the future held for the race. We must be prepared to meet the challenges and to accept opportunities when doors are opened to us. Responsibilities must be accepted and carried on without continual dependence upon others. These contemporaries often debated their philosophies regarding the roles people of their race would play in society, economics and governments worldwide. Both envisioned them as being future leaders in religion, society, education and government.

Ellen Gould (Harmon) White was also a contemporary of these men; however, she espoused a combination of both philosophies but in a broader sense. She counseled the training of the hand, head and the heart. She wrote:

"Our ideas of education take too narrow and too low a range. There is need of a broader scope, a higher aim. True education means more than the pursuit of a certain course of study. It means more than a preparation for the life that now is. It has to do with the whole being, and with the whole period of existence possible to man. It is the harmonious development of the physical (hand), the mental (mind), and the spiritual powers (heart). It prepares the student for the joy of service in this world and for the higher joy of service in the world to come.

"The world has had great teachers, men of giant intellect and extensive research, men whose utterances have stimulated thought and opened to view vast fields of knowledge, and these men have been honored as guides and benefactors of their race, but there is One who stands higher than they. We can trace the line of the world's teachers as far back as human records extend; but the Light was before them. As the moon and the stars of our solar system shine by the reflected light of the sun, so, as far as their teaching is true, do the world's great thinkers reflect the rays of the Sun of Righteousness. Every gleam of thought, every flash of the intellect, is from the Light of the world."—*Education*, pp. 13, 14.

The newly organized Seventh-day Adventist denomination initially took no steps to develop programs for the newly freed slaves. The leaders did build schools to train the children; however, Negroes and coloreds were not permitted to attend. Anna Knight in her book *The Mississippi Girl* tells of her dismissal from the Graysville School near Chattanooga when it was learned that she was a mulatto student. Thirty to forty years had passed since the church was recognized as an established religious organization, but its major thrust seemed focused on efforts to solidify its position in the religious community. Notwithstanding, the pleas by Ellen White to dedicate efforts for this downtrodden people, the leadership, headquartered in Battle Creek, Michigan, seemed content to use its time and resources in other areas. Missionaries were sent to distant lands to spread the gospel, and strong institutions were erected—hospitals, schools for their children, publishing houses to print literature, food factories, etc.

Battle Creek became the Seventh-day Adventists' colony to which the wealthy and famous retreated for fellowship, health treatment and relaxation. Ed H. Crump, the Mississippi-born political boss of Memphis, Tennessee, went there for treatment; he was not aware that one of his attendants was Anna Knight from Soso, Mississippi, his home state. Battle Creek became a paradise for the elite of the nation, and the church gloried in this recognition by world leaders.

The needs of the downtrodden people of the South still were not addressed by this "remnant" group. The prophetess carried a continual burden for these needs. She kept before the church its responsibilities and duties charged by God to help in this area. In the mid-1890s, she prepared ten articles for the *Review and Herald*, devoted especially to the work in the South. The first was published on April 2, 1895, while she was living in Australia. The other nine appeared in issues between November 26, 1895, and February of 1896.

Many years later, Mrs. White's son, James Edson, while returning with his younger brother, Henry, to Battle Creek from attending one of the Delaware Indian powwows, was eager to learn what he could about the Indian people and their relationship to the Seventh-day Adventist Church. He set out to find out all he could about anything that his mother, the prophetess, had said or written about colored people, but no one he contacted seemed to remember that she had said or written anything on the subject. Finally, a painter mentioned that he had seen such materials on the second floor in the Review and Herald Publishing House building and had been instructed by Uriah Smith, the editor, to discard the material. He had returned from placing the papers on the trash heap at the rear of the building. Edson repossessed the articles mentioned above and printed all but the first one in a book entitled *The Southern Work*. It was officially published by the denomination after Dr. Frank W. Hale, Jr., republished and distributed it in 1962 at the time of the General Conference session in San Francisco, California.

In the book, *The Southern Work,* one chapter is entitled "Our Duty to the Colored people." In it, the prophetess continually kept the needs of this field before the leaders. To get relief from her continued pleading, the leaders urged her to spend time in Australia giving guidance for the development of this newly organized field. She accepted and stayed in Australia for the next ten years, from 1890 to 1900; however, she never ceased to express her concerns for the colored people in North America.

Who were these colored people for whom she was so burdened and of whom she never ceased to speak? A look at Chapter 6 will give some insight. They were a mixture of the Moors (descendants of the Algerian, Moroccan and Spanish people), the Nanticoke Indians and other tribes with Europeans. Wherever Europeans went in the world, they seemed to have entered into mixed relationships with the people of that land. There were more than 500 Indian tribes, some of whom were the Aztec, Inca, Toltec, Algonkian, Sioux, Chicacoan, Nanticoke, Mohegan, Cherokee, Choctaw, Choptan, Wiccomiss, Ahatchwoops, Shawnee, and others. Included with these were Negroes, mulattos (mixture of European and African people), coloreds (mixture of Europeans and Indians), and various other persons of mixed ethnic heritage.

In C. A. Weslager's book *Delaware's Forgotten People*, an account is given of the colored people on this wise: "With the arrival of Europeans, their influences and leadership qualities, helped them to become the ruling groups in the new world. The natives were dispossessed of their land, their skills, their homes and moved to what we now know as 'reservations.' Although the natives banded together to drive the intruders out, it was too late. The tribes were disbursed to all parts of the continent. Some of the descendants of the Nanticokes refused to leave, as did some of the Cherokee tribe. The Nanticoke tribe roots led to the Scokum and Harmon people of Delaware. These intermarried with the Whites to produce a third raced—'colored people.' "

Ellen White had undoubtedly listened to ethnic slurs spoken by some of her associates in the church concerning these people, and even though she said little, if anything, about her own ethnic background, she often adamantly stressed the responsibility of the church to the colored people. Once she shared a vision concerning the work among the downtrodden race of the South. She is quoted in *The Southern Work* as saying:

"I know that that which I now speak will bring me into conflict. This I do not covet, for the conflict has seemed to be continuous of late years; but I DO NOT MEAN TO LIVE A COWARD OR DIE A COWARD, LEAVING MY WORK UNDONE. I MUST FOLLOW IN MY MASTER'S FOOTSTEPS. It has become fashionable to look down upon the poor and upon the colored raced in particular (at times it was difficult to distinguish mulattos from colored people). But Jesus, the Master was poor, and He sympathized with the poor, the discarded, the oppressed, and declared that every insult shown to them is as if shown to Himself. I am more and more surprised to see

MEMBERS OF THE NANTICOKE INDIAN TRIBE
AND THE MOORS

*Stephen Sockum,
Nanicoke store owner
who sold shot to
E. Lincoln Harmon*

*E. Lincoln Harmon,
Nanticoke counselor*

*Patrice Harmon,
Secretary, Nanticoke
Indian Association*

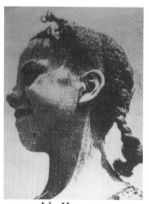

*Ida Harmon,
Nanticoke school girl*

*Levi Street,
Nanticoke farmer*

*Mrs. John Johnson,
Moor housewife*

Clem Carney,
Nanticoke farmer

George Carter,
Moor herbalist

Joseph Kimmey,
Moor carpenter

Winona Wright,
Nanticoke wife

Charles Clark,
Nanticoke chief

John Johnson,
Moor patriach, age 97

those who claim to be children of God possessing so little of the sympathy, tenderness, and love which activated Christ. Would that every church, North and South, were with the spirit of our Lord's teaching."—*The Southern Work*, pp. 10, 11.

It appears that some acceded a bit to accepting colored people into their ranks, but still felt that Negroes (mixed with African and European) would not be saved in the kingdom. Ellen White had stated in her book *Early Writings* that some of the slaves would not be resurrected to go to heaven when the Lord comes. To clarify this point, she stated in her book *The Southern Work*:

"The Black man's name is written in the book of life beside the White man's. All are one in Christ. Birth, station, nationality, or color cannot elevate or degrade men. The character makes the man, if a red man, a Chinese man, or an African gives his heart to God, in obedience and faith, Jesus loves him nonetheless for his color. He calls him his well-beloved brother. The day is coming when the kings and lordly men of earth would be glad to exchange places with the humblest African who has laid hold on the hope of the gospel. To all who are overcomers through the blood of the Lamb, the invitation will be given, 'Come ye blessed of my Father, inherit the kingdom prepared for you from the foundation of the world.'...The same price was paid for the salvation of the colored man as for that of the White man, and slights put upon the colored people by many who claim to be redeemed by the blood of the Lamb, and who therefore acknowledge themselves debtors to Christ, misrepresent Jesus and reveal that selfishness, tradition, and prejudice pollute the soul...God makes no distinction between the North and South. Whatever may be your prejudices, your wonderful prudence, do not lose sight of this fact, that unless you put on Christ, and His Spirit dwells in you, you are slaves of sin and of Satan.

"Why should not Seventh-day Adventists become true laborers together with God in seeking to save the souls of the Colored race? Instead of few, why should not many go forth to labor in this long neglected field? Where are the families who will become missionaries and who will engage in labor in this field?"—*Ibid*, pp. 12, 13, 27.

Ellen White also spoke of the need for the church to respond to the spiritual needs of the Chinese. Many Chinese were still living in America, having come in search of gold. Asian people were also being unkindly treated. Thomas Tsu-wee Tan in his book *Your Chinese Roots* makes this statement:

"Between 1840 and 1870, 40 million emigrants of all nationalities flooded into the United Sates which in turn caused industrial and social problems in the major entry cities like New York and Boston... In 1882, the Exclusion Act was the first federal attempt to limit immigration by nationality. These Chinese were selected as the main target even though the percentage of

Chinese arriving in America was very small compared to other nationalities from European countries...

"The Chinese were rumored to be overrunning the United States even though in actuality numbers were too few to pose a threat. Because of this fear and their imputed inferior status, they had to be kept out of America at all costs. The Chinese were felt as 'bringing filth, vice and disease,' and that every incoming coolie means...too much more vice and immorality injected into our [America's] social life.

"In a speech before the Joint Congressional Committee to investigate Chinese immigration in 1876, a witness described the Chinese in the following terms: [The Chinese] are inferior to any race God ever made. There are none so low. I believe that the Chinese have no souls and if they have, they are not worth the saving."—*Your Chinese Roots*, pp. 78, 82.

Africans, Chinese, Negroes, mulattos, Jews and Indians were not thought highly of even in Christian circles, but the gospel was for every nation, kindred, tongue and people, and Ellen White knew it. Part of her ancestral roots might really be traced to the Asian people who occupied this land in the year 1000 and became known as Indians. Through visions the prophetess spoke of appeals made to the Adventist leaders to share the gospel with these groups amidst their trials of life. She said:

"The Lord has looked with sadness upon the most pitiful of all sights, the colored race in slavery. He desires us, in our work for them, to remember their providential deliverance from slavery, their common relationship to us by creation and by redemption, and their right to the blessings of freedom.

"Some time ago, I seemed to be, during the night season, in a meeting in which the work in the Southern field was being discussed. The questions were asked by a company of intelligent colored people: 'Has God no message for the colored people of the South? Have they no souls to save? Does not the new covenant include them? If the Lord is soon to come, is it not time that something was done for the Southern field?'

" 'We do not,' it was said, question the need of missions in foreign lands. But we do question the right of those who claim to have present truth to pass by millions of human beings in their own country, many of whom are as ignorant as the heathen. Why is it that so little is done for the colored people of the South, many of whom are ignorant and destitute, and need to be taught that Christ is their Creator and Redeemer?

" 'Is it right for professed Christians to hold themselves aloof from this work allowing a few to carry the burden? In all your plans for medical work and foreign missionary work, has God given you no message for us?'

"Then He who has authority arose, and called upon all to give heed to the instruction that the Lord has given in regard to the work in the South. He said: 'Much more evangelistic work should be done in the South. There should be a hundred workers where now there is but one.' "—*Testimonies for the Church*, Vol. 7, pp. 223, 224.

As early as the 1870s, lay persons began responding to appeals made by the prophetess on behalf of these dear people caught in a web of involuntary servitude for hundreds of years. Wagon companies continued moving Westward in search of gold, and many former slaves joined the groups. The Midwest was a stopping place for thousands; in some instances, they went no further but remained and established towns in locations where the population was all Black. Others continued the journey Westward.

Pockets of Sabbath keepers were found among these groups, and soon the Adventist teachings had spread from Maine to California. Each group shared the good news with everyone they met. Joseph Bates worked in Michigan and New England; D. N. Canright also established the work from New England to the Pacific Coast. J. N. Loughborough preached from New England to Nevada. P. G. Rogers labored in California. A. T. Jones worked in California, Ohio, Michigan and Washington, D.C. The late Louvenia Mitchell of Oakland, California, often spoke of her parents' traveling over the Rocky Mountains and then settling in California, where they were baptized into the faith by Loughborough.

As early as 1873, Mrs. Henry VanSlyke and a group of believers established a school in Iowa to train colored children and adults. In later years their missionary zeal reached as far as the West Indies; they sponsored a young man named Joseph Hermanus Laurence of St. Kitts, West Indies, to attend the Huntsville Training School in Alabama in 1904. Another of their students, Thomas Branch, along with his family was one of the first missionaries to work among the people of Nyasaland and South Africa.

Another layman, Silas Osborne, heard of Adventism while visiting in Iowa and returned home to share these new biblical truths with former friends in Louisville, Kentucky. His family called him "Preacher" because of the speeches he made. Ten colored persons were baptized as a result of his meetings; this marked the beginning of the work among coloreds in Kentucky. However, it must be noted that Pastor Alonzo Barry, a Black Baptist minister who read of the teachings of the church in the *Review and Herald* had instructed the people and had them ready for baptism when Osborne arrived. Charles M. Kinney, a mulatto preacher, organized the group into an official body of the church in 1890.

J. C. Caldwell of Knoxville and Morristown, Tennessee, shared the "Word" with coloreds in East Tennessee and helped to establish the work in that area. Some of the first persons to accept the teachings came from the McBee, Hamilton, Thompson, Stephens, Graves, Slyger and Irvin families. When I became president of the South Central Conference, the clerk of the Probate Court in Morristown notified me that the Last Will and Testament of a White lady who lived in the area many years ago was probated in the courts. She had made provisions to help establish the Adventist work among the colored people of East Tennessee. More than 60 years passed before the estate was closed. The conference received funds with which to build a lovely house of worship in Morristown.

Not many years ago, the Last Will and Testament of Mrs. Frances Campbell Lynch, one of the original 16 students to attend the Huntsville Training School and who had also attended the Battle Creek School under Dr. J. Harvey Kellogg, was probated in Clinton, Tennessee, near the Smokey Mountains and an additional 31 acres were given for the advancement of the work among the colored people. The lay persons carried burdens to get the message to the colored people.

In 1873, E. B. Lane was sent from Indiana to officially establish the first church for colored people in Edgefield Junction, Tennessee, just 13 miles north of Nashville. Lane reviewed the new truths with the people (Black and White) while standing in the doorway between "Black" and "White" waiting rooms at the train station; however, the church really had its beginning with Pastor Harry Lowe, a Baptist minister who brought Sabbath keepers together in 1873. Some who joined were the Allison family and their foster son, Samuel J. Thompson, another of the original 16 students to attend the Huntsville Training School in Alabama when it opened its doors in 1896.

Other lay persons who labored for the colored people in the South were P. T. Magan, E. A. Sutherland, Nellie Druillard, James Edson White and Judge J. Price Pearson. Some who joined Edson with his mission was a group of colored leaders from the state of Delaware, including John Street, Frank Warnick, and his daughter Naomi, the mother of the Simons children, Norman, Donald, John, Richard, Raymond, Betty and Lois, most of whom also became leaders in the church.

At the turn of the century, Elder E. E. Frank, a Seventh-day Adventist leader, began to evangelize the colored people of Delaware and in the Eastern part of the country. Here is the record:

"About forty-five years ago, one of the band (Cheswold Moors/Nanticoke Indians) named Frederick Seeney, a son of James Seeney (mentioned in earlier chapters), attended a tent revival meeting at Kenton conducted by Elder E. E. Frank, a White Seventh-day Adventist minister. Frederick Seeney was moved to embrace the new faith and, fired with zeal, he set out to convert others of his people. He did baptize P. G. Rogers. Frederick, like Russell Clark (the original Nanticoke Indian leader), was a natural leader, but his efforts were poured entirely into religious channels. The Seeney family was the first to break away from the existing church ties and to follow their relatives in accepting this new faith. Later, members of the Moseley, Durham, and other mixed-blood families received the Adventist faith. A church was erected called

DESCENDANTS OF THE NANTICOKE AND MOOR PIONEERS

Frank W. Warnick

*Emma (Taylor) Warnick, wife
of Frank W. Warnick*

*Frederick H. Seeney, pioneer
Seventh-day Adventist among
the Nanticoke Indians*

*P. G. Rogers, convert of
F. H. Seeney*

the Forest Grove Church, on the western approach of Cheswold, and missions were eventually established in other parts of Pennsylvania.

"The separation of the Adventists from the Methodist Church provoked minor ill feelings for a time between the two church groups. One of the Methodists spoke of the Adventist religion as having 'broke out about forty years ago' as he might refer to a malady. One primary distinction between the two sects is that the Adventist observe their Sabbath on Saturday and do not consider Sunday a holy day. The Methodists hold their church services on Sunday, while on that day the Adventists go about their regular tasks. The difference in Sabbath observance caused perceptible friction at first in view of the strict Methodist attitude toward Sunday...

"The Adventist Church is considered a colored church, although its membership does not contain Blacks. At this writing, it has about 40 members. The Manship and Fork Branch Churches are also termed 'colored' churches, although their membership consists of Moors. The term 'colored' is used to mean non-white, but not necessarily Negro. Most of the Moors admit that they

DESCENDANTS OF THE NANTICOKE AND MOOR PIONEERS

Raphael Warnick,
son of Frank W. Warnick

Marie Warnick,
wife of Raphael Warnick

Glen Simons and wife Naomi (Warnick) Simons,
daughter of Frank W. Warnick

DESCENDANTS OF THE NANTICOKE AND MOOR PIONEERS

Ellen G. (Harmon) White

Nanticoke Indian school

*Nanticoke school children. The new generation, like the old, exhibits
a wide range of facial types and skin color.*

Oscar Sammons, Jr.

Herbert Sammons

Mildred Sammons,
Moor bride

Fred Hughes,
Moor farm hand

The old Nanticoke church building in
Cheswold, Dleaware

are colored but are angered if even by inference someone designates then as Negroes. To them, a colored person is not White, but he is not necessarily a Negro. All Negroes are colored persons, but not all colored persons are Negroes."—*Delaware's Forgotten Folks*, pp. 143, 144.

So the Seventh-day Adventist members heeded the pleas of the prophetess and began sharing the biblical teachings of Adventism with colored people. They became the leaders of the church in that sector and in turn began to open its doors courageously and to accept all nations, kindred, tongues and people into the faith. These tended to follow the same practices of their fellow members of the Colored Methodist Episcopal Church.

Durhams can be found in Kentucky; Morgans in Virginia and Alabama; Clarks and Johnsons in Michigan; Cokers in Indiana; Streets, Jacksons, Harmons and Hills in Delaware and Pennsylvania and Burtons in California and Tennessee.

From small beginnings the Lord has continued to smile upon the work done to fulfill the church's duty to the colored/Negro people in the North American Division, as well as to other people in all corners of the world.

Mrs. Richard Norwood and her family. The children's father is a grandson of Sameul Norwood, a former Nanticoke leader. The mother was born a Harmon.

Present day Norwood S.D.A. family

Chapter 15

Charles M. Kinney—The Morning Star Of Black Adventism

"How beautiful upon the mountains are the feet of him that bringeth good tidings, that publisheth peace, that bringeth good tiding of good, that publisheth salvation, that saith unto Zion, thy God reigneth." Isaiah 52:7

Charles M. Kinney was born a slave in Richmond, Virginia, in 1855. He was eight years of age when slavery came to an end and was one of the millions who wandered from place to place in search of his family roots and of a place that he could call home. He joined a wagon train that was headed West and finally reached Reno, Nevada, where he found employment and settled in to put his life together. While there, he attended evangelistic services conducted by J. N. Loughborough, accepted the Seventh-day Adventist faith, and became the first Black member of the Reno, Nevada, church. After two years' attendance at Heraldsburg College (1883–1885), he entered the colporteur ministry of the Seventh-day Adventist denomination.

Ellen G. White and other leaders of the church saw great promise in Kinney and encouraged him to devote his life to the service of God. Later, he was sent to Wichita, Kansas, where he established the work among the few colored believers there. From Kansas, his ministry took him to St. Louis, Missouri, where he surprisingly found some unpleasant relationships existing among the races. Blacks were not allowed to attend services where Whites were in attendance. They were not even allowed to witness Kinney's ordination to the gospel ministry. These attitudes were carried over from racial strife and a court decision that took place in Missouri before freedom came. Kinney took the church leaders to task about the situation, but it was to no avail.

From St. Louis, he was sent to Louisville, Kentucky, where a group of colored people had accepted the teachings of the church after being instructed by Alonzo Barry, a lay preacher who had convinced them of the truthfulness of the biblical teachings of the Seventh-day Adventist faith.

While traveling through Kentucky on his way to his new responsibility, he sold books to pay for the trip, since no financial assistance had been provided to meet his expenses. Two places where he worked were in Hickman and Mayfield, Kentucky. When he arrived in Hickman, he found himself at the home of Robert and Martha Talley. This couple regularly gathered their sons and daughters around them to thank the Lord for delivering them from the slave institution under which they had lived until Robert reached the age of 47 and Martha was 19. Their sons Gentry, John, Nathan and Albert had also been born slaves and had experienced forced labor. Oppression had been awesome, the living conditions unbearable. Only the grace of the Almighty had helped them to endure these rigors. But now they were free.

On August 8, 1863, the news concerning their freedom finally reached their western Kentucky hometown. Many who had been slaves came together and began to dance in the streets and to thank the Lord for His loving kindness. He had not forgotten their pleas and their prayers for that better day. Each year after that, the grandchildren and the great grandchildren would return to this part of the South where the good news was first heard.

On that eventful day, they sang and danced up and down the dusty roads from dawn and all through the night. The rejoicing was heard all over western Kentucky, from Hickman to Paducah, to Mayfield, to Union City, to Dyersburg, to Hopkinsville. "We'se free! We'se sho nuff free!"

Uncle Nathan said that they sang and danced all night and onward through the following days. They sang songs of thanksgiving until they were completely exhausted.

Free at last! Free at last!

Thank God Almighty, we'se free at last!

Been to the mountain, been to the mountain;

Thank God Almighty, we'se free at last!

When I get to heaven, I'm gonna sing and shout;

Thank God Almighty, I'm free at last!

Ain't nobody there can turn me out!

Thank God Almighty, I'm free at last.

The Emancipation Proclamation that had been signed January 1, 1863, and was now the law of the United States stated:

"Whereas, on the twenty-second day of September, in the year of our Lord, one thousand eight hundred and sixty-two, a proclamation was issued by the President of the United States containing, among other things, the following, to wit:

"That on the first day of January, in the year of our Lord, one thousand eight hundred and sixty-three, all persons held as slaves within any State or designated part of a State, the people whereof shall then be in rebellion against the United States, shall be then henceforward, and forever, free and the Executive government of the United States, including the military and naval authority thereof, will recognize and maintain the freedom of such persons, and will do no act to repress such persons, or any of them, in any efforts they make to their actual freedom.

"That the Executive will, on the first day of January aforesaid, by proclamation, designate the States and parts of States, if any, in which the people thereof, respectively, shall then be in rebellion against the United States; and the fact that any State, or the people thereof, shall be on that day be in good faith represented in the Congress of the United States by members chosen thereof at elections wherein a majority of the qualified voters of such States shall have participated, shall, in the absence of strong countervailing testimony, be deemed conclusive evidence that such State, and the people thereof, are not then in rebellion against the United States..."

This edict brought joy to the hearts of Robert and Martha Talley and their sons, and they settled in the country with their 40 acres of land and a mule that had been provided for them in the freedom contract. The family lived on the land in an area known as "the bottom," and each year when the Mississippi and Ohio Rivers overflowed their banks, they were forced to seek higher grounds until the water subsided.

The last set of their children were born free—Robert, Jr., Carrie, James and Julia. Julia was my mother. The first and second sets of children had felt the pangs of slavery, but now all were blessed to pursue life, liberty and happiness. The parents taught each one to serve the Lord and to appreciate the liberty that had come to them.

Hickman was popular because of its river trade. Boats frequently stopped there to load cotton and other crops for transport to Cincinnati, St. Louis, Paducah, Memphis, Vicksburg, Greenville, Natchez and New Orleans. In 1904, Ellen White, the prophetess, wrote concerning this part of the South:

"There are cities in the South—New Orleans, Memphis, St. Louis— in which but little has been done, and there are others that have not been entered. In these places, the standard of truth is to be entered. With might and power we are to carry the truth to the people."—*Manuscript 56, 1904.*

C. M. Kinney carried a burden for these unentered areas and went from place to place telling people of One who had not only freed them from bondage, but had also freed their minds, bodies and souls from sin and its penalties. His mission was challenging, but it brought satisfaction to his own heart as he told the story from town to town, village to village and city to city.

While going about her chores one afternoon, Grandma Martha saw what appeared to be a White man walking toward their home. Many thoughts began running through her mind, as she mentally reviewed the abuses that White people had inflicted upon her people, the Cherokee nation. She was tempted not to be hospitable, but her Christian principles compelled her to receive the man with kindness.

"Many White Americans acknowledge the agrarian skills of Cherokee, Chicasaw, Choctaw, Creek and Seminole—as well as their adoption of European customs—dubbing them the Five Civilized Tribes of the Southeast. Yet the settlers' desire for more farmland overcame their admiration. They demanded that the Indians go. President Andrew Jackson responded by signing the Indian Removal Act of 1830, setting the stage for a saga the killing exodus along the 'Trail of Tears'—Thousands of Indians had perished because of sickness, the winter weather, and mental anguish of this 'death march' from the Carolinas to Oklahoma.

"A minority faction of Cherokee agreed to the emigration of the entire nation by signing the Treaty of New Echota in 1835. But news of calamities suffered by other tribes being forced West strengthened the resolve of some Cherokee to stay on their ancestral land, but many were killed and their land taken from them...by the time the last exiled Cherokee arrived in Oklahoma in 1839, the forced march had claimed as many as 4,000 lives."—*National Geographic*, Vol. 187, No. 5, p. 86.

These were Grandma's relatives. In spite of the past history concerning the trials the Cherokee nation had passed through and lingering reflections, she gave a cordial greeting to this stranger who had come to her door, especially when she discovered that Kinney was a person of mixed blood as Grandpa was. She listened intently as he explained his mission. Kinney was selling the books *Bible Footlight* and *Bible Readings for the Home Circle*. Grandmother was eager to learn to read and seized the opportunity to purchase the books so that she could learn about all of the things that had been denied the family during the days of slavery.

By reading the books, she taught herself to read and to understand the Bible and other books. As her reading improved she discovered many truths that she had never heard before. In her thirst for learning, she was convinced that the family had been worshiping the Lord on the wrong day. She shared this gem with her family, cherished it in her heart and instilled it in the hearts of her children until she died. Although she continued to serve the Lord religiously on Sunday, the seed had been sown, and in later years, Julia, her youngest daughter and her grandchildren became members of the Seventh-day Adventist faith. The book salesman whom she had met turned out to be Charles M. Kinney, who was on his way to Louisville to fulfill his mission to organize a congregation of colored people that became the Magazine Street S. D. A. Church.

For a time, Kinney's base of operation was Mayfield, Kentucky, not far from Murray, Kentucky. From Mayfield, he walked to nearby communities selling books and spreading literature like the leaves of autumn. He went to Paducah, Fulton, Hickman, Murray, Kentucky, Union City, Tennessee and to surrounding areas in Western Kentucky and Tennessee; however, he never worked in Memphis. He not only sold books, but invited people to become members of the church he represented. Because of his ethnic background, he could move freely among both races of people. Race relations were very good in Kentucky following the Civil War. His ministry changed the lives of many and drew many from the popular churches. This angered the ministers, and they sought to destroy his works by rumors that were untrue; however, the Lord stood with him. In Murray, Kentucky, he baptized T. M. R. S. Howard, who later became one of the most outstanding surgeons to graduate from the Huntsville Training School and Loma Linda Medical College.

When Charles M. Kinney finally reached Louisville in 1890, he found ten persons who had joined the church under the preaching of Alonzo Barry. In this group were the Minnis and the Slaughter families. Miss Emma Minnis was ten years old when the message came to Louisville; she accepted it and remained true to the faith until her death.

Louisville, Kentucky, located on the banks of the Ohio River was one of the border states during the Civil War. The state had not been totally pro nor anti-slavery. Fairly good relationships existed between master and servant. Tobacco and corn crops and river trade were some of the principal industries that required little slave labor. Cotton was not king as it was in the states farther south.

From a religious standpoint, Louisville had served as the host for the Methodist Episcopal, South, denomination when the issue over slavery divided the Methodist Church into two groups. Much race mixing had taken place in the state, and mulatto and colored people could be found in abundance. It was in Louisville that William Henry Miles, a mulatto and the second bishop of the Colored Methodist Episcopal Church, was born. Now, another religious light had been placed in the community by the Seventh-day Adventist Church. The Seventh-day Adventist Church in this city today is historically the oldest colored church of the denomination in the entire world. Kinney organized the congregation on February 16, 1890.

In giving a sequence of the establishment of other colored churches in the South, Elder Kinney outlined them as follows:

One year after the organization of the Louisville congregation, on June 13, 1891, he was directed to go South about 100 miles to Bowling Green, Kentucky, to organize another company of believers. This company included the parents of Luther Milligan and family members who had come to a knowledge of the biblical teachings of the church. The message was going before Kinney, and the Lord was using him to establish these new converts officially as a part of the denomination.

On September 15 and 16, 1894, he was sent to organize a congregation in Nashville, Tennessee, with nine charter members, including the Allisons, Jordans, Thompsons, Lewis, Crudas and others. From Nashville, he was sent to New Orleans to organize a group that had been attending meetings held by T. B. Buckner. Some of the founders here were the Washingtons, Scruggs, Scales and some few others. He had finally reached the city that the prophetess had seen in vision as needing to hear the gospel. During the same year, churches were established in Birmingham, Alabama, where the Finley and Pearson families lived. Another organization took place in Lexington, Kentucky, that same year. It is understandable why Charles M. Kinney was named the Morning Star of Black Seventh-day Adventism.

In 1894, Elder Kinney went to Huntsville, Alabama, in search of a suitable site on which to establish a school for the training of the children of former slaves to share the gospel message with their own people. When Elders Olson and Butler arrived from the General Conference, he carried them to this area that had served as the Jacobs plantation before the Civil War.

It was also a historic site, for Andrew Jackson, one of the presidents of the United States, had made many visits to the Old Mansion for festive occasions; Dred Scott, the former slave, had served on this plantation for more than 18 years. He was one who helped to change the direction in history when the courts of Missouri denied him his freedom. This was a meaningful location. Ellen White stated that this was the very spot that the Lord had shown her in vision and that it would serve as a place for the training of Black youth. It was here that the Huntsville Industrial Training School (presently Oakwood College) was established in 1896.

Kinney was a dedicated leader of his people and sought to serve them and his God in many areas, so that all who desired to obtain salvation was given an opportunity.

Charles Kinney married Shirley Hodnet in Nashville, Tennessee, but ceased from active duty with the church when she was overtaken by illness which lasted for many years. He retired in Nashville as a resident of the Riverside Sanitarium and Hospital. He lived to be a ripe old age after he had been used by God to help establish the work of Adventism among Black people across the land. He passed away in 1951 and was buried in Greenwood Cemetery. Elder Eugene Carter officiated at his last service. His wife preceded him in death.

He was born a slave in Richmond, Virginia, in 1855, but when emancipation from slavery freed his body and the gospel of Jesus Christ freed his soul, he went forth on a mission for God. He demonstrated vision, conviction, courage, determination, forthrightness, dedication to duty, compassion and a burden to see his people ready to meet the Lord when He finally returns for His church. Charles M. Kinney was the "Morning Star of Black Adventism."

We have seen the Lord lead this people from before the cross, through centuries of enslavement to a historic emancipation, allowing them to chose freely the paths that they deemed best for them.

"*THOU WHO HATH BROUGHT US*"

The Development of the
Seventh-day Adventist Denomination
Among African-Americans

Book One
Volume Two

"*Climbing Up the Rough Side of the Mountain*"
1863–1900
"God of our weary years, God of our silent tears
Thou who hath brought us thus far on our way
Thou who hath by Thy might lead us into the light
Keep us forever in the path, we pray."
—James Weldon Johnson

By
Charles E. Dudley, Sr., D. D., L. L. D.

Tamar Henley Corry, Editor

"THOU WHO HATH BROUGHT US"
The Development of the Seventh-day Adventist Denomination
Among African-Americans

Climbing Up the Rough Side of the Mountain

Book One - Volume Two

Table of Contents

Foreword

A youthful shepherd carried his sheep from the valley to the top of the mountain to graze. He soon discovered that the sheep did not survive. An experienced shepherd counseled the lad that he would have better success if he would carry the sheep half way up the mountainside, allow them to reproduce, then carry the little ones to the top. The African-American forefathers did not enjoy the good life that the present generation enjoys, but with hope, vision, determination and concern about those who would follow them, they never gave up in the struggle for equality for their people. They wanted their offspring to share the better things of life that others enjoyed in this world and then to realize the heavenly blessings promised on the other side of life.

After enduring 400 years of enslavement in the New World, African-Americans began experiencing the long-prayed-for freedom, only to realize that this new life was not going to be easy. Although granted 40 acres of land and a mule by the government, they still were compelled to make many adjustments. They had to learn to compete in society, to succeed in business endeavors, to achieve new educational goals, and to rely on God. In facing these challenges, these people came to realize that life was like climbing a mountain with very little equipment with which to make the journey to the top. However, they were determined to succeed in this challenging venture. It would take centuries and sometimes death, but they would never give up the struggle. They would never lose sight of their objectives in climbing the rough side of the mountain of life, and they would never turn around. With each generation, the objective was always the same.

When climbing the 19,340 foot Mt. Kilimanjaro in Africa, the guide has climbers to begin making the journey during the night. One of the reasons for this, we are told, is that climbers beginning the climb during the daylight hours often become fearful when they look back and see from whence they have come. When they see how much farther they must climb, they often become discouraged and give up. To reach the top, one must have a vision of what can be. There must be hope, trust, patience, determination, confidence, holy boldness and sometimes defiance for the obstacles along the way. Such has been the struggle of African-Americans in their efforts to achieve success in this new life of freedom.

What is the goal? Pastor Wintley Phipps sings, "We're climbing up the rough side of the mountain, climbing up for to see my Lord." Before and after the Civil War, our fore-parents often spoke and sang of their "mountain-top experiences." They were taught that the Lord ofttimes meets His people on mountain tops. He met Abraham on Mt. Moriah (Genesis 22:2–12), and three times on different mountains, He met His servant Moses—on Mt. Horeb, He revealed His presence and gave him a commission (Exodus 3:1); on Mt. Sinai, He gave His law (Exodus 19:1–5); and on Mt. Nebo, after Moses had seen the promised land and had died, He buried him in a tomb before resurrecting him and carrying him to glory to live forever (Deuteronomy 34:1–6).

Moses climbed up the mountain just to get a view of the promised land. His trials, challenges, burdens and regrets all ended with the Mt. Nebo experience, and he became satisfied that his struggles on earth had been worth it all, especially after the Lord gave him a panoramic view of the awaited blessings.

In more recent times, Dr. Martin Luther King, Jr., the great Civil Rights leader of the 1960s, in his last sermon before his death, told his people, "I have been to the mountain and have seen the promised land, I may not get there with you, but we will get to the promised land!"

African-Americans are acquainted with the struggles through which they must pass to enjoy the better things of life here and hereafter. These struggles have been many and continuous in the past, but the mountain climbers have persisted and will not cease until they achieve success.

This group in the Seventh-day Adventist Church has endured many trials in an effort to be recognized as an integral part of the church body. Attitudes of leaders within the church during its infancy appeared to deny them this right. After the Civil War, little thought was given to inviting this downtrodden people to become a part of the group. But being led by God, they read the Bible and the church's publications and organized themselves into small Sabbath-keeping groups. The leaders still did not extend open arms; nevertheless, the Lord blessed these believers with spiritual gifts, and their numbers grew, as did the Hebrews in Egypt, until they were recognized as being a part of the body. This did not end the problems, however; the struggles became endless.

Segregated practices in the church have existed for years. Differences in the roles, careers and opportunities for leadership open to African-Americans when compared with those open to other ethnic groups are very distinct. African-Americans were compelled to establish their own programs and institutions. The struggle to climb up the rough side of the mountain to success has never ceased.

In this volume, we will address issues surrounding the establishment of the Black church within the Seventh-day Adventist denomination in America, acceptance of Blacks into church membership, establishing centers of operation for Blacks across the country, the opening of church schools to train the youth to serve their own people, and the training of doctors to minister to the people and to help with the expansion of the work across America.

Slaves sang songs of endurance and hope in climbing the mountains of life. The more determined they became, the more they excelled, and the Lord led them each step of the journey. During and following the days of slavery they sang, "I'm climbing high mountains, trying to get home!" When they reached what appeared to be the mountain top, they realized that other experiences would bring them from that peak to another valley. They took courage when they saw another mountain loom before them; it was then that they would sing "Lord, don't move this mountain, just give me the strength to climb it."

The transition years from 1863 to 1900 were just as challenging for the freed men and women who had been subjected to bondage for so long as the challenges facing every mountain climber. In the face of many disappointments, rejections, burdens, problems, unfair treatment and practices and community problems, they remained undaunted while climbing the rough side of each new mountain. There was no discharge in the struggle. They must keep climbing until the goal is reached.

Chapter 16

The Emergence Of S. D. A. Groups Under Black Leadership

"Let the work be managed so that colored laborers will be educated to work for their own race." Testimonies for the Church, Vol. 9, p. 202

Long before Seventh-day Adventist leaders began to share their faith with African-Americans, Black people had begun to teach their own people the biblical truths held by the church.

Many accepted the seventh-day Sabbath and believed that the imminent return of Jesus to earth for His waiting church was significant for their salvation. Some had been active in the Millerite Movement, the precursor to the Seventh-day Adventist Church. John W. Lewis, a preacher of another persuasion preached the Millerite message with fervor. Charles Bowles, the son of an African woman and a Revolutionary War officer, preached to thousands before his death just before the "passing of time" in 1843.

"It was William E. Foye who, no doubt, made the greatest contribution. Foye, a mulatto, who at that period could have influenced either White or Black, under spiritual duress, recounted visions in 1842 that God gave to Ellen G. White. It takes but a cursory reading of the writings to see this, and Mrs. White admitted their relationship. He, however, 'let his color become his crossing' and stopped giving the message. Foye said of William Miller that Miller did not care for people who spoke of having visions and dreams and that he (Miller) did not care for people of his (Foye's) color.

"When no particular work was done to get them to become a part by the church leaders, Negroes, free and in the North did join the Adventist Church. They mingled with the White membership and because of this, it is hard to trace them. We do know that the first Sabbath-keeping Adventist church, in 1844, in Washington, New Hampshire, did have Negroes in attendance and listed as charter members when it was organized.

"There was no organized work among Negroes in the North or South before the Civil War, the General Conference was not organized until May 21, 1863, when the war ended, and the Emancipation Proclamation was signed by President Lincoln. Eight years later in 1871 the first call came from the South that eventually led to the establishment of the first Negro S. D. A. church. It was from R. K. McCune and a few other Whites who had accepted the message through some tracts and then sent a request to Battle Creek for a minister to come and instruct them."—*North American Informant*, November–December, 1971.

In 1871, Adventists began working among African-Americans. In March of that year, E. B. Lane, a church leader from Indiana, responded to the call and held a series of meetings in Edgefield Junction, Tennessee, just 13 miles north of Nashville. When Negroes showed up for the meetings, he seated them in the telegraph room. By standing near the door, he could speak to Whites gathered in the main hall, as well as to Blacks in the telegraph room at the same time. Interestingly enough, his wife proved to be a more convincing evangelist than he, and through her ministry, along with his, many were added to the church.

The *North American Informant*, a paper published by the Negro Department of the General Conference, stated: "When the meetings ended the few Negroes who accepted the teachings sat, as custom was, in the rear of the group and remained thus for more than a dozen years. In 1883, they and few others were organized into a company at Edgefield Junction, Tennessee now under Elder Harry Lowe. Lowe had been convicted through Lane's teachings at the original railroad station meetings, but had become a Baptist minister. A tract on the Sabbath helped convert him now as a licentiate minister. *The S. D. A. Encyclopedia*, page 724 says, 'probably the first Negro American S. D. A. Minister,' he was given charge of the company.

"We must not confuse the commentary statement, for it further states that no date for his ordination has been found. Charles M. Kinney, therefore, is called the first ordained Negro S. D. A. Minister on page 665 of the same commentary, so there is no confusion."

Elder Harry Lowe organized the group composed of Blacks and Whites into a company in 1883. However, The *North American Informant* further stated: "On November 9, 1886, this group was organized as the first Seventh-day Adventist Church composed entirely of Negroes. Its first offering of fifty cents was given in its entirety to missions. Participating as charter members were the Jonathan Allisons whose two sons became ministers—Thomas H. Allison, known for his musicianship and preaching in the South and Midwest, and Jonathan Allison, Sr. who worked in the South and West. J. W. Allison, Jr. also pastored in the Midwest and at the University Boulevard Church in Los Angeles."—*North American Informant*, November–December, 1971.

The other two children of Father and Mother Jonathan Allison were Florence and Herbert, both of whom became teachers. Florence moved to Los Angeles, married Pastor M. Brawley, a Baptist minister, and taught music in the public school system for more than 50 years. Unfortunately, disappointing racial circumstances arose among the church leaders, and she left the church, never to return. Herbert became the principal of the high school in Clarksville, Tennessee. His life came to a mysterious and tragic end after he allowed Seventh-day Adventists to use the school to conduct evangelistic meetings for the community. This was very displeasing to the citizens of the community.

The Allisons brought two other young men with them to the services from week to week—Samuel J. Thompson, a foster son, and Levi Watkins,

PIONEER OF THE FIRST CHURCH AT
EDGEFIELD JUNCTION, TENNESSEE

E. B. Lane, teaching at the railroad station

Lillian (Boggs) Carter and husband; she is a descendant of W. E. Boggs, church pioneer.

Father and Mother Johnathan Allison and family

Thomas H. Allison

Florence (Allison) Brawley, daughter of Johnathan Allison

The late Levi Watkins, former president of Alabama State College in Montgomery (as a child, he attended Sabbath services with the Allisons).

PIONEERS OF THE COLORED WORK

John Green, \Sr.

Sydney Scott

M. C. Strachan

John Mann

C. M. Kinney

L. C. Sheafe

Johnathan Allison, Sr.

J. Gershom Dasent

Alonzo Barry

J. H. Laurence

F. H. Seeney, J. H. Laurence, M. C. Campbell, G. E. Peters, J. G. Dasent

131

the son of a Baptist family—who were their nearby neighbors. Thompson was also one of the original 16 students to enter the Huntsville Training School in 1896, but he never became a minister in the organized work. After leaving the Huntsville school, he became a stalwart leader in Knoxville and served until his death. His wife, Mary, a sister to Sally and Rachel McBee of Knoxville, was also one of the 16 students to attend the school.

Although his father insisted that he never join this new faith, Levi Watkins was a sympathizer of the faith until his death. In the later years of his life, Watkins became a teacher and finally served as the president of the Alabama State College in Montgomery, Alabama, until his retirement.

Another family at Edgefield Junction was the Boguses. William Bogus was married to Ella Bogus; they had one son, Ernest, also a member of the church. William Bogus, Jr., later changed his name to Ernest William Dixon after his foster family, who were also members of the Edgefield Junction group. Lula Walker Dixon, the foster mother reared William Ernest Bogus with her children. Ernest, now a member of the church, married and became the father of four children, Lillian, Ernest III, Wesley and Catherine. Lillian, Ernest III and Catherine became members of the Seventh-day Adventist church in later years. Today, Lillian is the wife of a publishing director of the South Central Conference, Robert Carter. Catherine is married to Joseph Herbert of Murfreesboro, Tennessee. Ernest was the first elder of the Edgefield Junction group.

The oldest predominantly Black congregation in existence in the entire world is the Magazine Street Seventh-day Adventist Church in Louisville, Kentucky. Two men—one African-American and one White—are thought to have had an impact on the beginning of this congregation. Silas Osbourne, the first Seventh-day Adventist known to work among the colored people of the South, taught his former slaves with the hope that the biblical truths would help them serve God better and would aid them in their preparation to meet the challenges of life. His preaching followed the efforts of Alonzo Barry, an African-American, whose efforts among his own people resulted in the baptism of ten persons who became the founding fathers of the church in Louisville. Among the group was the Emma Minnis family. Miss Minnis taught music in the school system for more than 50 years. The church was one of the most musically talented congregations in the Seventh-day Adventist denomination.

Just before the turn of the century, Pastor Louis C. Sheafe organized the first Seventh-day Adventist congregation, consisting of persons of all races, in Washington, D. C. However, when the General Conference headquarters moved from Battle Creek to the Washington, D. C., area following the unquenchable fires that leveled the buildings in Battle Creek, White members withdrew from the First Seventh-day Adventist Church and organized a segregated congregation in Takoma Park, Maryland, where Blacks were not allowed to attend. Elder Sheafe expressed his disappointment to Ellen White over this segregationist action. To his dismay, she advised him to preach to his own people until such time that he would be able to preach to White people.

In *Testimonies for the Church*, Volume 9, p. 199, Ellen White wrote: "Instead of wondering whether they are fitted to labor for White people, let our colored brethren and sisters devote themselves to missionary work among the colored people. There is an abundance of room for intelligent colored men and women to labor for their own people. Much work remains to be done in the Southern field. Special efforts are to be made in the large cities. In each of these cities there are thousands of colored people to whom the last warning message of mercy must be given. Let the missionary spirit be awakened in the hearts of our colored church members. Let earnest work be done for those who know not the truth." Elder Sheafe never completely recovered from this counsel.

In recounting the history of the First Seventh-day Adventist Church of Washington, D. C., former pastor of the church Melvin Hayden recorded:

"The very first Seventh-day Adventist congregation in the nation's capital was organized February 23, 1889 with 26 charter members. In January of 1866, Elder Willard H. Saxby and wife, a Bible instructor of Vermont, were the first converts in Kentucky and began a ministry of sharing the faith with the unreached. They were assigned to Washington, D.C., to establish new work for the denomination. Elder Charles Parmele and his sister, Julia, of Illinois and others including apprentice Bible instructors, such as Miss Mary Senator, the mother of the Graham children of Chicago, went throughout the city giving Bible studies to anyone who showed an interest in the Seventh-day Adventist biblical teachings. This group operated a city mission at 1831 Vermont Avenue in Northwest Washington. During the first three months they gave 297 Bible studies and gained one convert. In two years they had a Sabbath School of 46, which, having outgrown the Vermont Avenue location, they began meeting in Claybough Hall at 1630 Fourteenth Street, N. W. After worshiping at the location for three years, they were organized into the First Seventh-day Adventist Church of Washington, D.C., on February 23, 1889 by Elder John O. Corliss. During the following weeks the church was visited by Elders Uriah Smith, L. McCoy and others.

"Elders J. S. Washburn and Charles Taylor held a series of evangelistic meetings in 1890, and in 1893 a small building was purchased. The congregation was interracial and among its members was Mrs. Rosetta (Douglass) Spragg, daughter of the renown abolitionist, Frederick Douglass. Dr. Eva B. Dykes and her uncle also became members of this church. Among the speakers who addressed the members during the period was Ellen G. White, the prophetess, whose prophetic gifts and voluminous writings have been a constant encouragement and guide to Adventist believers around the world."—Letter from Elder Melvin Hayden, Pastor of the First Church of Seventh-day Adventists, Washington, D. C., 1954.

Evangelism continued to be uppermost in the hearts of these believers, and the membership among colored people grew; other churches were formed as a result of the growth.

Ellen White counseled the students at the Huntsville Training School in 1904 to work for their own people. Her words to them, as recorded by Anna Knight in her book *Mississippi Girl* were: "We need, oh so much, colored workers to labor for their own people in places where it would not be safe for White people to labor. This is why we have established our printing office (the Southern Publishing Association in Nashville). You can labor where we cannot, in places where existing prejudice forbids us to labor. God wants the colored students in many places where White workers cannot labor."—*Mississippi Girl*, p. 212.

These words gave strong encouragement to many to work for their own people. Then the work began to develop through strong evangelistic efforts by men such as L. C. Sheafe, John Manns, Sidney Scott, J. K. Humphrey, J. H. Laurence, G. E. Peters, P. G. Rodgers, M. C. Strachan, T. B. Buckner, J. M. Campbell, M. G. Nunez, J. G. Dasent, B. W. Abney, Sr., H. D. Green, and Thomas and Jonathan Allison.

One student who responded to Mrs. White's appeal was Joseph Herman Laurence from the island of St. Kitts in what was then the British West Indies. Laurence, who had been rejected by his Episcopal preacher father, was able to attend the Huntsville school through the generosity of two White ladies in Iowa, who heard of his plight and decided to sponsor the young man. He later married into the "well-to-do" Brandon family of the Brandontown community near Huntsville, a few miles from the Huntsville Training School. He along with his bride took up work in the heart of Mississippi where James Edson had labored at the end of the nineteenth century aboard the Morning Star boat.

Laurence encountered numerous difficulties laboring in Mississippi, Louisiana and Tennessee, not the least of which was a lack of adequate funds to care for the financial needs of his family. When Ellen White and other women of the church learned of Laurence's plight, not uncommon among colored workers and poor Whites, these women sent their tithe to support the workers. This action brought criticism from C. F. Watson, president of the Colorado Conference. In response to his rebuke, Ellen White wrote him a letter dated January 22, 1905. In it she stated:

"It has been presented to me for years that my tithe was to be appropriated by myself to aid White and colored ministers who were neglected and did not receive sufficient money to support their families. When my attention was called to aged ministers, White and Black, it was my special duty to investigate into their necessities and supply their needs. This was to be my special work, and I have done this in a number of cases. No man should give notoriety to the fact that in special cases the tithe is used in that manner.

"In regard to the colored work in the South, that field has been and is still being robbed of the means that should come to the workers in that field. If there have been cases where our sisters have appropriated their tithe to the support of the ministers working for the colored people in the South, let every man, if he is wise, hold his peace."

While working in Mississippi, Laurence's wife became ill and passed away; however, after her death, he was transferred to Denver, Colorado, where he continued a very productive ministry among the colored people. He later married Geneva Questley Wilson, and to this union six children brought joy to the family. The names of the children were, Hermanus, Genevieve, Jocelyn, Dorothea, Mae Eloise and Carty.

Even before Laurence or James Edson began working for the colored people in Mississippi, a colored man by the name of Alonzo Parker, a creole preacher from Louisiana, crossed the Mississippi River at Vicksburg and proclaimed that Jesus would return to earth for His church in the not-too-distant future and that the seventh day of the week, or Saturday, was the Lord's Sabbath, the true day of worship for Christians to observe. The colored people of Mississippi became angry because of his teachings and beat him mercilessly. He fell in the streets of Vicksburg and died at the scene. As his life was ebbing away, he placed his Bible upon his chest and prophesied to them, saying: "In about one year, the Lord will give you another chance to hear and accept this gospel in Vicksburg." The seeds of truth had been sown, and exactly one year later, in 1895, James Edson White took his Morning Star boat to that city and began teaching the same gospel.

At the turn of the century, Elder John Manns and his brother, Charles, outstanding evangelists whom the Lord used to bring hundreds into the faith, questioned why so much money was being given by Black people and very little returned to help the work among them. He was reprimanded by the leaders. Subsequently, he withdrew from the organized work and began setting up his own churches in South Georgia and Northern Florida. He named his group the "Free Seventh-day Adventist Church." He carried hundreds of members with him when he withdrew, and scorned those who did not join with him by accusing them of still being in slavery.

Throughout the United States, the work among colored people has experienced many drawbacks, challenges, problems, trials and difficulties, but the Lord has been with the dedicated workers who learned to endure hardship without grumbling. Despite obstacles, the membership in the North American Division of the Seventh-day Adventist Church continued to be blessed by God in a signal manner.

In Volume 9 of the *Testimonies for the Church*, page 225, Ellen White wrote the following:

"Although much remains to be done for the colored people, we have cause for rejoicing over the good beginning that has been made. In a recent number of *The Gospel Herald* [1907] it is reported that 'fifteen years ago [1892] there were not over twenty colored Seventh-day Adventists south of the Mason and Dixon's line; but today there are seven hundred. Twelve years ago, there was only one colored Seventh-day Adventist church; today are fifty, not counting those in Africa and the West Indies. . . The tithe of the colored people last year in the United States amounted to five thousand dollars, fifteen years ago it was not over fifty dollars.' "

For years, records have been kept concerning the growth of the work among all peoples of the church. It is interesting to watch how the Lord has continued to finish His work among every nation, kindred, tongue and people and especially among African-Americans. Glory, glory, hallelujah, His truth keeps marching on. When church leaders did not seem to show an interest in opening their doors to African-Americans, the Lord raised up leaders among them to lead them courageously up the rough side of the mountain to receive the message of His love.

Chapter 17

The Beginning Of The Work In Kentucky

Seventh-day Adventist teachings among African-Americans in the states of Tennessee and Kentucky met with ready acceptance, although not in as large numbers as it did farther south in Mississippi and Alabama, the "Cradle of Adventism." The first congregation involving African-American members was established, as stated earlier, at Edgefield Junction, Tennessee, in 1883. But the first Black congregation was established in Louisville, Kentucky, in 1890, to be followed by another in 1892 in Bowling Green. Other groups were established in Lexington in 1894, and in New Orleans, Louisiana, and Birmingham, Alabama, during the same year; another was established in Paducah, Kentucky.

By 1900, according to Ellen White, there were about 50 African-American Seventh-day Adventist members in the entire world; most of them lived in the state of Kentucky. Today, approximately 2,000 members worship each week throughout the state. Today, congregations are found in Covington, Campbellsville, Frankfort and Ft. Knox. Others once existed in Richmond and Berea but, regretfully, these congregations were closed when the members died or moved to other areas.

Kentucky is an industrial center between the North and the South and was considered a border state during the Civil War. Kentuckians took a moderate stand on the slave issue when it divided the two factions into separate camps placing family against family, brother against brother; the effects of which exist until this day. Many slaves here lived better than some Whites in other parts of the country. The relationship between the master and slave was somewhat cordial. Many slaves were used as house servants; this exposed them to family and community business, which others were not privy to hear, at home and in the work place.

Slaves accepted their status as slave/servants, and there were many that resulted from mixed-blood unions throughout the state. Harriet Beecher Stowe's *Uncle Tom's Cabin* depicts the trust that many slaves had in the master, and vice versa. It speaks of a trusted slave living in the "big house" in Paducah, who was sent alone to sell wares to the merchants across the Ohio River into Cincinnati. In crossing the Ohio River, Tom was in free territory; he could have kept going, but he returned with the money, which amounted to as much as $5,000.00 at that time, to his life of slavery. It did not enter his mind that inasmuch as he was on the other side of the Ohio River, he was technically a free man. Many of his fellow slaves longed to cross the river into

THE BEGINNING OF THE WORK IN KENTUCKY

C. M. Kinney

People of Hickman, Kentucky who listened to Kinney's preacheing.

Thomas Chapel C. M. E. Church in Hickman, oldest Black church in Kentucky

Pastor Warren Thomas, one of the original sixteen freed slaves who established the church

Mrs. Luther Milligan & Mrs. Alfonso Bean of Bowling Green Church. Milligans' parents were founders of the church.

N. C. Wilson, president of the General Conference visits with Miss Emma Minnis, one of the first ten baptised in Louisville in 1880

The Colored SDA Capmeeting in Kentucky in 1920

freedom, but dutiful Tom returned to his master in Paducah with the money from the sale of the merchandise. Unfortunately, when a financial crisis arose for his master, Tom was sold to masters in a predominantly cotton-picking state, where he experienced hardship, persecution and trials that eventually led to his death.

Some White people who lived in Kentucky had serious problems accepting the institution of slavery; they felt that the system of slavery was not acceptable to God and raised their voices in protest. Stephen Foster, who was born in Florida near the Swanee River and later settled in Kentucky, depicted the plight and experiences of the slaves when he wrote: "My Old Kentucky Home," "Old Black Joe" and "Carry Me Back to Old Virginy." The masters and their families loved to hear the darkies sing these songs and others of their own creations which spoke of the hope these heaven-bound slaves had. The songs were also codes that gave instructions for escape.

Harriet Tubman, the run-away slave who led hundreds of her fellow slaves to freedom, often sang some of these songs as she made her "missionary journeys" for the cause of freedom.

Pastor Henry Ward Beecher, a minister of the Methodist Church, became very active in the programs to put an end to slavery. Julia Ward Howe who was also a member of the abolitionist movement and the Underground Railroad set to music the oft sung song "The Battle Hymn of the Republic" which said, "I have seen Him in the watch fires of a hundred circling camps; they have builded Him an altar in the evening dews and damps. I can read His righteous sentence in the dim and flaring lamps, His truth is marching on."

"The Methodist Episcopal Church at the time of their General Conference in 1844 expressed grave concerns over the slave issue; this led to a division in the church, resulting in the Methodist Episcopal and Methodist Episcopal, South. The delegates from the annual conference in the slaveholding states met in Louisville, Kentucky."—*United Methodist of America*, p. 84.

Many slaves remained members of this church until 1870.

The Seventh-day Adventist Movement was coming into being when this division took place. Ellen Gould Harmon, the spiritual eye of the church, along with a number of the new denomination's leaders were former Methodists. In her book *Early Writings* she stated:

"At the age of eleven years I was converted and when twelve years old was baptized and joined the Methodist Church. At the age of thirteen, I heard William Miller deliver his second course of lectures in Portland, Maine."

Ellen G. White spoke of angels taking part in the Civil War battles. "Just then an angel descended and waved his hand backward. Instantly there was confusion in the ranks. It appeared to the Northern men that their troops were retreating, when it was not so in reality, and a precipitant retreat commenced. This seemed wonderful to me. Then it was explained that God had this nation in His own hand, and would not suffer victories to be gained faster than He ordained."

Abraham Lincoln, a Kentuckian, was born on February 12, 1809, on a farm near Hodgenville. He took no liking to slavery and is purported to have said: "If the opportunity ever presented itself, I will hit this and hit it hard." On January 1, 1863, as president of the United States of America, he signed the Emancipation Proclamation which ended slavery; however, this action cost him his life.

Religious activities on behalf of slaves were nurtured in Kentucky. The Methodist Church had a stronghold in the state during the early days of its organization, and many slaves with religious convictions held Methodism as their religious persuasion. The first two Black bishops of the Colored Methodist Episcopal Church were William H. Miles, a mulatto of Louisville, Kentucky, and Richard Vanderhorst from Charleston, South Carolina. Vanderhorst passed away just two years after be became bishop, but Miles served for a number of years, and a number of churches and institutions of the denomination were named in his honor.

At the end of the Civil War, the official organization of the Colored Methodist Episcopal Church was established in 1870 in Jackson, Tennessee; the church spread to many parts of the Southland. The parents of Alex Haley became members in Hennin, Tennessee, 50 miles north of Jackson. My grandparents, Robert (Doc) and Martha Talley, were among the founding leaders of the church in Hickman, Kentucky. It was established in 1890 and named for Uncle Warren and Aunt Sallie Thomas as the Thomas Chapel C.M.E. Church.

The following news report by the Associated Press in 1992 gave an account of this history of the Thomas Chapel C.M.E. Church from its beginning:

"According to tradition, the church got its start on Palm Sunday in 1866. Warren Thomas and his wife, Sallie, were attending a service at a church that allowed Blacks only in a segregated section. Sallie Thomas was caring for a White family's four year old son during the service when the boy dashed to the front of the church. When she tried to grab him, she bumped into a former Confederate army captain, who pushed her to the floor.

"After the incident, Blacks were excluded from the church and on Easter Sunday, 1866, the Rev. Warren Thomas, first delivered a sermon to a small group of former slaves in a shack near the Mississippi River.

"The first meetings of the Black church were held at the shack, but in 1896, Thomas guided the former slaves to build the original Thomas Chapel C. M. E. Church with hard earned farming money. This was the beginning of the Colored Methodist Episcopal Church in Hickman, Kentucky."—*Associated Press*, 1992.

Robert and Martha Talley were among the original 16 members that formed this church in Hickman. The original building has been designated by the state of Kentucky and the City of Hickman as a historical monument. It is the oldest Black church building in the state.

One notable family in Hickman was that of Pop and Annie Atwood. They had seven children. Rufus Ballard Atwood, the sixth child, developed an interest in education and an appreciation for the finer things of life. He served his country during World War I and in later years became the president of Kentucky State University in Frankfort from 1929 to 1962, a period of 33 years. Dr. Atwood was from the C. M. E. Church in Hickman.

Another of Hickman's sons was Albert Gaynes Thompson, born in 1910. He was a minister of the African Methodist Episcopal Church in Laporte, Indiana, but converted to the Seventh-day Adventist faith in 1929 after listening to the preaching of Joseph H. Laurence in South Bend, Indiana. Thompson was my brother. Regrettably, his ministry with Adventism was brief. After five years in its service, he passed away at the youthful age of 28 while pastoring the Beacon Light S. D. A. Church in Kansas City, Missouri. Little did the family realize at that time that his younger brother, Charles Dudley, would be called of God to help finish the ministry that he had begun.

Other family names representative of the membership of the Seventh-day Adventist Church in Kentucky were McNichols, Miles, Harbor, and Travis in Paducah. At one time there were more than 125 members with African ancestry in the church there. Some of the pastors were J. H. Wagner, Sr., Frank L. Bland, C. Sampson Myles, Lee A. Paschal, Ricardo McKinney, Joseph W. McCoy, Wallace J. Mitchell, Willie S. Lee, Jr., Raynard Allen and William Pergerson.

Some of the members in Lexington were the Bibbs, the Stewarts, the Custards, the Saulters, the Westbrooks and Sister Grace Frazier, founder of Adventist church and school to the south of Lexington. The Walker family established the church in Richmond.

In 1938, Charles M. Kinney presented to Dr. Otis B. Edwards of Oakwood College, the following chronology of the first official outreach efforts of the Seventh-day Adventist Church to the colored people:

1. November 1887—Edgefield Junction church was organized with nine members.

2. February 16, 1890—Louisville church was organized by R. M. Kilgore with ten charter members. (This was the first Black congregation organized in the denomination and the oldest in the entire world).

3. June 13, 1891—the Bowling Green church was organized by C. M. Kinney with eight charter members. Among these members were the parents of Luther Milligan who was born after his parents became Seventh-day Adventists. (Some of the pastors who served there were W. J. Cleveland, Dr.

C. A. Meyers, Sr., J. Richardson, C. David Joseph, Doc C. Hatcher, Lee A. Paschal, Albert Frazier and William O. Freeman.)

4. June 4, 1892—New Orleans, Louisiana, church was organized by C. M. Kinney with ten charter members. (Some of the members were the Washingtons, the Bennets, the Scales and the Scruggs.)

5. September 15, 16, 1894—Nashville, Tennessee, church was organized by C. M. Kinney with nine charter members. (Some of the families were the Jordans, the Lewises, the Allisons, the Boguses.)

6. Fall of 1894—Elder James Edson White began work in Memphis, Tennessee, after being arrested by city authorities for using Finis Parker, a colored pilot from Indiana, who had no license, to sail a boat in those waters. After remaining there for a period of time, he proceeded onward to Vicksburg, Natchez and Yazoo City, Mississippi.

7. June 19, 1896—Birmingham, Alabama, church was organized by Elder Hottel with 15 charter members, among whom were Judge Price Pearson and his family and his sister, Mrs. Elzira Finley.

These constituted the total African-American congregations of the Seventh-day Adventist denomination with the exception of the church in Washington, D. C. Establishing the work among this people was challenging, but their leaders continued climbing up the rough side of the mountain with vision and determination to share the message of God's love and saving grace to other African-Americans.

Chapter 18

African-Americans' Struggles During The 1880s

As long as Ellen White was alive, she kept Seventh-day Adventist leaders reminded of the church's duty to the colored people in America. She emphasized this continually until it appeared that she was urged to move to Australia to help with building up the work there. She remained in Australia for ten years (1880–1890), but struggles of Blacks within and without the remnant church continued and their efforts to find a place in the expanding work of the church never ceased to be a challenge to its leaders.

An unwelcome attitude against African-Americans prevailed everywhere. Inside or outside of the established churches, colored people suffered greatly during the post Civil War years. Even church leaders were guilty of ruthlessness and violence against this people; however, when the prophetess returned to America, she continued revealing visions and dreams from the Lord concerning the work among this people. Changes in the relationship among the races needed to be made, and this was not going to be easy. Often there was a total disregard for her counsels. She then wrote pamphlets concerning "Our Duty to the Colored People," which were cast aside until they were discovered on the trash heap by Edson White and published in a book entitled *The Southern Work.*

Around 1889 and 1890, Jesuit missionaries/priests of the Catholic Church began streaming into the United States (the New World) and making their influences felt across the land. About the same time, the Ku Klux Klan, consisting of Protestant White men in Pulaski, Tennessee, was formed in opposition to (1) African-Americans because of their new social status as equals and the political gains they had made, (2) Jewish people because of their business acumen and leadership strengths (the blessings that God pronounced upon Abraham was still with them), and (3) Catholics because of the religious persecutions that they had inflicted upon Protestants during the period from 538 to 1798.

By 1890, many of these former slaves began settling in the North, which they felt was "the land of promise," only to discover that conditions there were no better than in the South and often worse. Large numbers of these suffering pilgrims were found in St. Louis, Chicago, New York, Washington, D. C., and Philadelphia. When moments of despair and depression came, they were comforted and encouraged by songs of hope by Charles Albert Tindley (1853–1933), a Methodist minister in Philadelphia. Pastor Tindley's ministry helped the people to hold to the promises of God and inspired them to trust in God to help them through the storms of life.

He was blessed of God to build the Tindley Memorial Methodist Church's membership from 100 to 10,000 before his death. Vongoethe Lindsay who later served as the first secretary/treasurer of the South Central Conference of Seventh-day Adventists was one of his members, as were Duke Ellington, the Mills Brothers and Marian Anderson. At the age of 80, he admitted himself into a hospital in Philadelphia. When asked why he had come, his response was, "I came to die!" He passed away within two weeks.

His hymns told of experiences from slavery to this time. Some are still being sung in congregations across the land such as: "Take Your Burden to the Lord and Leave It There," "Nothing Between My Soul and the Saviour," "When the Storms of Life Are Raging, Stand By Me" and "I'll Be All Right Someday."

Another who later strengthened the hopes of this people was Thomas A. Dorsey. He was born in 1891 and lived in Chicago, where he settled after leaving New Orleans, Louisiana; Jackson, Mississippi; Memphis, Tennessee; St. Louis, Missouri; and other parts of the South leading North. He also gave additional assurance to the people with his songs. His music changed the worship atmosphere in the entire African-American community. "Just a Closer Walk with Thee" and "Precious Lord, Take My Hand" were among his compositions.

"Gradually, the popularity of Black gospel spread from the church and individual performers; writers of vaudeville and blues began to switch to gospel performing and writing. Thomas A. Dorsey (1899–1993) is by far the most famous of this group. He began to compose gospel songs while performing occasionally in the blues and vaudeville circuits. His first gospel hit was, 'If you see my Saviour, tell Him that you saw me.' "—Songs of Zion, p. 173.

About this time, President George I. Butler and other leaders of the Seventh-day Adventist Church began to be more sensitive to the needs of African-Americans. On her return from Australia, Ellen White, the prophetess, continued to stress that changes in the church's relationship with African-Americans were necessary, and she urged the leaders to address the needs of the colored people of the South. In 1894, Charles M. Kinney was asked to find a suitable site where a school for the training of coloreds could be established. A school for White youth had been established at Graysville, Tennessee, but coloreds could not attend. The A. S. Steel School for these youth had been established in nearby Chattanooga, and literally hundreds of students, including Trula Wade, Grace McDonald, W. J. Cleveland and F. S. Hill, were trained there.

In search of a new location, Kinney was led by the Holy Spirit to journey south to the town of Huntsville, Alabama, where he discovered an old slave plantation that he deemed appropriate. When the owner, Mr. Solomon Jacobs, agreed to sell the plantation for the establishment of that school, Ku Klux Klan members assembled at the site with the intent of inflicting bodily harm to Mr. Jacobs. However, the presence of "guards" posted at the gates thwarted their attempts. The "guards" were believed to have been angels watching over the green acres where African-African workers would be trained to share the gospel with their people. The Lord was guiding in the affairs of men.

When A. V. Olson and I. H. Evans visited the site, they agreed that it was very ideal for the intended purpose and recommended that it be purchased. There were over three hundred giant oak trees on the land. It was a historic location. Andrew Jackson had often visited it from the Hermitage Plantation in Tennessee. Dred Scott, the Missouri slave, had spent 18 years working there before being taken to Missouri. It had been an auction place for slaves, and the auction block remained on the campus for many years after the school was established. Students would walk over it on their way to their classes. Now, it was going to be God's "green acres."

Not long after the school was established, some of the church fathers suggested that the project be canceled and the property sold, claiming that it was a financial drain on the church. However, when Ellen White visited the site in 1904, she stated that it was the very spot that the Lord had shown her in vision and demanded that not one acre of the land be sold. This was the beginning of Oakwood College.

Chapter 19

The Work Of The Church In Memphis, Tennessee

"The Lord gave a message to Brother..., instructing him to take up the work in Memphis... He obeyed the word of the Lord, and he has reported excellent success in his work in Memphis." Evangelism!, p. 398

Memphis was a key city for the spreading of the gospel among African-Americans, not only in America but throughout the world. After slavery ended in 1863, large numbers of former slaves settled in the area—some who had helped to make cotton king in these parts during slavery remained to work the land in the tri-state area consisting of West Tennessee, Northern Mississippi and Northeast Arkansas; others followed the path of the railroad in search of loved ones, many of whom had settled in Memphis. This city was a rest stop where slaves passed on their way North to freedom. African-Americans' presence in the city left many historical landmarks, one is the auction block where slaves were sold at the corner of Auction and Main Streets.

Memphis stood at the crossroads. Memphis was a great railroad center, according to Fred L. Hutchins in his book, *What Happened in Memphis?* Two railroad stations, the Central and the Southern Railroad were there. Before the railroad era, steamboats were used to carry freight, as well as passengers. Among the well known boats that served Memphis were the Lee Line steamers—the Robert E. Lee, James Lee, Stacker Lee, Georgia Lee, Ora Lee, Sadie Lee, Rowena Lee, Reece Lee, Peters Lee, Harry Lee, also the Fred Herald and the Chicksaw.

Incidentally, Charles and Sadie Lee were prominent, colored socialites of Memphis who became members of the Seventh-day Adventist Church. Charles Lee was one of the stabilizing influences of Adventism in the city, along with Emma R. Jones, Melissa Smith, Jennie Weir, Callie Weir, Callie Taylor, Lizzie B. Jeter, Dorothy Kent and A. J. Nash.

Memphis became a center for the growth of African-American business, one of which was the Lee Line, mentioned above. Joseph Edison Walker, who worked his way from poverty through Meharry Medical College in Nashville to become a physician, businessman and philanthropist founded the Universal Life Insurance Company in Memphis. The business has since become one of the five largest Black-owned companies in the United States.

Joseph Catron was a well-established businessman living in the Avalon Community who extended his furniture moving business all over the city. He became a member of the Seventh-day Adventist Church and often was the sole financial supporter of the church in Memphis.

Robert Seard, Sr., was born in Memphis and owned the only Black house moving business east of the Mississippi River when he moved his business to Greenville, Mississippi. For years, his influence was felt throughout the state of Mississippi; it was he whom God used to advance the work of the church in the state for decades.

Mary Church Terrell was born in Memphis during the same year of the Emancipation Proclamation and devoted her entire life to fighting for equality for all people. A writer, lecturer, organizer and demonstrator, she was active in the successful efforts to desegregate restaurants in the nation's capital; however, eating spaces in Seventh-day Adventist facilities remained segregated for decades after others were made accessible to everyone in that city.

William Christopher Handy (1873–1958), the son of a Methodist preacher in Tuscumbia, Alabama, settled in Memphis and organized a band. All of his life he had heard the secular songs of despair, of love, of hope, of longings, which lightened the daily lives of Black farm hands, wash women and laborers. Handy became known as the father of the blues; however, his work was not limited to blues. Among his more than 150 compositions is the African-American Hymn "Blue Destiny," a symphonic piece. One of his best loved sacred hymns "Give Me Jesus" is to be found in the current Seventh-day Adventist Church Hymnal.

Sister Lucy Campbell, a public school teacher in Memphis and leader of the Women's Auxiliary for the National Baptist Convention, was a composer who made many contributions to Black religious music sung in Black churches across the nation. Through many of her hymns she told of Black experiences and cultures. Her compositions that will live forever are: "He'll Understand and Say Well Done," "Precious Memories," "Something Within Me." Her last days were spent in the S. D. A. Riverside Hospital in Nashville, Tennessee.

Mrs. Pearl M. Crawford, another public school teacher in Memphis for more than 50 years, was a member of the Seventh-day Adventist Church. She also held the distinction of having been one of the original members of the Fisk Jubilee Singers in Nashville, who in the fall of 1870 sang before the kings and queens of the earth, and before President U. S. Grant, his White House staff and other elite of America. (The singers introduced Negro spirituals to society and received gracious acceptance.) In her witness to her community on Dunlap Street in Memphis, Mrs. Crawford influenced Earnest E. Rogers to attend Oakwood Junior College in Huntsville, Alabama. He became a minister for the Seventh-day Adventist Church and spent a lifetime training students to become leaders in the church.

Jennie and Edris Stratton were born in Georgia but moved to Memphis early in life and joined the Seventh-day Adventist Church. Jennie became one of the sweet singers in Israel. She later married Harry Dobbins of Jacksonville, Florida, and served on the teaching staff at Oakwood Junior College in

PIONEERS AND DESCENDANTS OF THE SDA WORK IN MEMPHIS, TENNESSEE

Mrs. Ella (Cunningham) Gray, matriach

Mr. Isaac Gray, patriach

Mrs. Emma R. (Gray) Jones

Harry Gray

Pearl Gray

Charles Gray and wife, Ruth (Maycock) Gray

Irene Williams (granddaughter)

Mrs. Rose Gray and children

MEMPHIS, TENNESSEE

Mississippi Boulevard Welfare workers

*J. E. Walker, Sr.,
founder of
Universal Life
Insurance Co.
of Memphis*

*Joseph Catron,
SDA pioneer*

*Mrs. Pearl Crawford,
one of the original Fisk
Jubilee Singers and
SDA member*

*Robert Seard,
the only Black house
mover east of the
Mississippi River,
but moved to
Greenville Mississippi.*

*Mrs. Jennie Stratton
Dobbins of
Memphis—became a
part of the staff at the
Huntsville School.*

Huntsville, Alabama. Edris married Milton M. Young, another minister of the church.

Adventism began in Memphis during the winter of 1894–1895 with W. R. Reed who held a series of meetings for two months. C. L. Boyd, the president of the Tennessee Conference of Seventh-day Adventists, held cottage meetings in 1894 resulting in the organization of a church of seven members. V. O. Cole and his wife were among the charter members, and their home became the first meeting place for the congregation. Two years later they moved the congregation to a rented room at the corner of Main and Beale Streets. Later, the members bought their own building at the corner of Dunlap and Faxon Streets in 1900 at a cost of $1,000. Very few, if any African-Americans were members of this congregation at the time.

The relationship among the races was cordial after the Emancipation, but tensions soon began to mount and by 1866, race riots had broken out. After that, racial tensions grew worse and by the turn of the century, strong racial barriers existed; even in religious circles, Blacks and Whites did not worship together. The Adventist work among African-Americans began here in 1906 when literature evangelists from the denomination's Review and Herald Publishing Company in Battle Creek, Michigan, arrived in Memphis selling books in the Black community. Ella Gray, a colored lady who lived in the rural community of Frazier, purchased some of the books. After reading them she began to adhere to the teachings of the church. She also taught her family what she had read.

Because of severe racial tensions, Mrs. Ella Gray chose to establish a mission in her home in Frazier rather than worship with the White congregation at Dunlap and Faxon Streets. Her witness led many in the community to join her in keeping the Sabbath, and the group continued to grow in number until the house could no longer accommodate the congregation. Larger quarters were sought and several locations were used until the members finally settled on a house located on Mississippi Boulevard at Jennette Street in South Memphis.

From these humble beginnings, the work among African-Americans in Memphis had world-wide impact as its members scattered to make contributions to society and to the church. Some who held membership in the church in Memphis included Joseph Catron, the mover, and his family; Alma Manus, a real estate broker; Charles Lee who served as the first elder of the local congregation until his death, along with his wife Sadie and daughter Evelyn; and Louis H. Bland, Sr., who became a part of the organized work and pastored congregations in Tennessee, Louisiana, Michigan and New York City, where he finally became the first president of the Northeastern Conference of Seventh-day Adventists, a position he held until his death. He and his life-long friend, Charles Lee, were working together in the railroad shops in Memphis and were baptized into the Seventh-day Adventist Church at the same time. It is sobering to know that both men died on the same day—one in Nashville, the other in Memphis.

Mrs. Alice Humble came from a large farm in Mississippi to enroll her daughter Audrey in the Seventh-day Adventist church school where Mrs. Emma Gray Jones was the teacher. The lessons that the young girl learned while in attendance at the school helped her and her mother to become members of the Seventh-day Adventist Church. Mrs. Callie Weir, another socialite from the community, along with her two daughters, Melissa and Jennie, and her son, Andrew, also joined the church. These early members were taught by L. H. Bland.

And then there was Mrs. Jennie Taylor, the mother of John and Daniel, who became a staunch believer of the faith. Mrs. Hattie Jones joined and brought many of her twelve children with her.

A very colorful lady of prominence in the city, Mrs. Lizzie Bell Jeter, was another baptized member; as were Joseph and Verna Ward from New Orleans, Louisiana. Brother A. J. Nash, a very fair-skinned man, was baptized and became a dedicated member in the Lord.

The congregation grew significantly under evangelists and pastors who came to serve. Solid ecclesiastical guidance was given by a number of spiritual leaders, among whom were J. H. Laurence, Sidney Scott, W. B. Mallory, J. Wisdom Jones, Louis H. Bland, Sr., and Fred S. Keiths.

The story is told that Keiths was challenged to a debate by one of the pastors of the Church of Christ. He informed the pastor that he had no desire to debate him; however the pastor insisted and made his challenge public. Keiths requested that the event take place in the Church of Christ building. When he arrived, many inquired where his members were. "They could not come tonight," he replied. Keith was designated as the lead-off speaker. He stood and gave a strong message on the Sabbath, put on his coat and left the room. The pastor charged: "It is not fair." But Keiths had given his message and was gone.

Since those early days of the work in Memphis, other ministers have been used by God to build upon the foundation laid by the forerunners. Today, over a half million African-Americans live in this city. Ironically, it has an African-American mayor and many city officials of color serve in government. This younger generation continues to build upon the foundations laid by the forefathers with their blood, sweat, tears, prayers and dedication. These are influencing cities, nations and people in and out of the Seventh-day Adventist denomination around the world. The city is known as "Memphis, Down in Dixie."

The river boats still dock at the foot of Beale Street, and many people still gather to "wheel on Beale"—not just Blacks, but people of all ethnic backgrounds. The corner of Main and Beale Streets is where the Seventh-day

Adventist members gathered to worship from Sabbath to Sabbath; the Tri-State Bank is now located there. Memphis is still the home of the famous Cotton Carnival. Cotton is shipped all over the world from this city.

Memphis, the home of Lemoyne-Owens College, the home of the Colored Methodist Episcopal Church, the home of the Church of God in Christ; Memphis, the home of the Tennessee Medical Center; Memphis, the home of the largest lumber center in the world; Memphis, one of the gateways to the golden West; Memphis, the pathway from New Orleans in the South to St. Louis and Chicago in the North; Memphis, where more churches than service stations are found; colorful Memphis, Tennessee. Many other industries can be found here, but thank the Lord that Adventism is also alive and well in this community, and it is flourishing among all races and nationalities and people. This Memphis is the city that Ellen White saw in vision and the place where she instructed the leaders to establish a work for God among the people.

The Seventh-day Adventist work among Blacks in Memphis had its beginnings in the home of Mrs. Ella Gray who purchased books from a literature evangelist and began to teach her findings to her children Emma, Harry, Pearl, Rose and Isaac. Emma was sent to the Huntsville School in Alabama for training and became the first church school teacher for African-Americans in the Adventist church in Memphis. Harry was sent to Vicksburg, Mississippi, in 1912 to be educated with students from the Morning Star boat. Rose went to Vicksburg to teach in the school but became ill and had to return to Memphis where she later died. Harry later also attended the Huntsville School in 1922 and later went to Chicago and became the president of the Musicians' Guild. Charles A. Gray the son of Isaac attended Oakwood in 1922 and later taught school in New Orleans, Detroit and Indianapolis. Pearl married and settled in Chicago where she remained until her death.

The work in Memphis has grown significantly since its humble beginning. Today, five congregations are witnessing for God at Longview Heights, Word of Faith, New Covenant, Overton Park, Breath of Life and Collierville. Other outreach ministries have begun in nearby cities in Northern Mississippi, Arkansas and West Tennessee. The members continue to climb the rough side of the mountain toward the goal.

Chapter 20
Acceptance Into S. D. A. Membership

Small groups of African-Americans had begun keeping Saturday as the day of worship and were living in expectation of the second coming of the Lord, even though little effort was put forth by leaders of the church to share the biblical teachings with them. It was not until the General Conference session of 1887, held in San Francisco, California, during the second term of George I. Butler, that the issue was put on the floor for discussion and to be voted on. By this time, about 10 persons of African heritage held membership in the church. But small groups adhering to the teachings of the church were found in various places, and the number of believers were increasing.

According to an article in *Adventist Heritage Magazine*, Spring, 1985: "During the course of the meeting a lively discussion centered around the denomination's attitude toward 'the color line.' Elder A. T. Jones advocated that no color line be recognized, that is, that no racial prejudice be allowed in the church. A minister from Tennessee (R. M. Kilgore), responded that if a pastor in his state should try to mix the races in church he would end up with no White members. Another minister offered a resolution that this conference recognize no color line. An animated discussion followed, pro and con. One opinion held that we should take things just as we find them, not arousing any unnecessary prejudice...leaving the Spirit of God to obliterate the color line in the hearts of those who may be converted by the truth."

This was a difficult question for the newly organized church, especially against the background of the social, religious and political conditions prevailing in the country. This disenfranchised race of African descendants whose forefathers had been enslaved for more than 400 years was now experiencing some of the blessings of freedom. Some had become city officials, congressmen and businessmen; many were church leaders. They had received support and had experienced some political, social, financial and educational growth under U. S. President Ulysses S. Grant, during the reconstruction days. However, when Rutherford B. Hayes followed Grant as president, he ended the 12 year reconstruction period, removed all federal troops from the South, appointed a southern democrat to the Cabinet, and took a hands-off federal policy regarding southern political affairs. The results were a reversal of many of the milestones that African-Americans had realized and mounting racial tensions increased among all Races.

Feelings of resentment and outrage against African-Americans because of the small successes they had achieved led to Jim Crowism, segregation, violence, riots and bloodshed. The influence of the recently organized Ku Klux Klan spread across the South and across the land, instilling fear in the hearts of even some Seventh-day Adventists.

Separate houses of worship were already in existence among the Methodists and Baptists in the South. The A. M. E., the A. M. E. Zion, the C. M. E., the National Baptist and the African Baptists organizations were separate from the other Methodist and Baptist organizations in the South. African-Americans were not allowed to attend the places of worship that Whites attended. This practice extended even to some localities in the North.

Given these factors, the decision on whether to accept these people into the worship experience of the Seventh-day Adventist Church became a real heart-searching challenge for the group. Alfonso T. Jones was particularly articulate in his call for full church membership for everyone. He was a young, bold and outgoing preacher whose sermon delivery had the style and flavor of traditional African-American preaching. He was thrilled whenever he had the opportunity to speak to a Black congregation and was inspired by their involvement during the course of his sermon. Jones' motion to accept people of all ethnic backgrounds into church membership was rejected. However, church leaders voted instead to refer the matter to a committee consisting of Uriah Smith, Ellet J. Waggoner and Archibald R. Henry for study. The committee never brought a recommendation to the floor for consideration. The motion to accept all races of people into membership in the church was never brought for discussion again.

During the following year, it was A. T. Jones who became one of the leaders of the historic 1888 Movement in the Seventh-day Adventist denomination. This movement addressed another question on righteousness and "justification by faith." Strong positions were taken during the meeting of 1888, and following the meeting, division and widely differing points of view tended to surface in the church, finally leading to the dismissal of A. T. Jones from church membership. He was reinstated in a Black church in Washington, D.C., by F. H. Seeney. Church leaders were outraged and troubled that Seeney had allowed Jones to rejoin the church and disciplined him (Seeney) for doing so. However, A. T. Jones remained a member of the Black congregation until his death in 1923.

On the issue of membership for African-Americans in the Seventh-day Adventist church, however, *Adventist Heritage Magazine* noted that "after conferring with those who had worked in the South and finding them unanimously agreed that our work could be done without creating a disturbance of neglecting colored people, the committee saw no need for the session to legislate on the matter and recommended that no action be taken and that all references to this question be omitted from the minutes. The recommendation was adopted, but the matter was not laid to rest, for it would surface again at the 1962 session of the General Conference held in San Francisco."

DEBATORS FOR ADMITTING COLORED INTO SDA CHURCH MEMBERSHIP—1887

C. M. Kinney

R. M. Kilgore

Delegates to the General Conference in San Francisco, California—1887

A. T. Jones

J. Harvey Kellogg

In 1962, Dr. Frank W. Hale, Jr., Mylas Martin and Burrell Scott assembled the Black delegates to the General Conference at the Jack Tarr Hotel in San Francisco and told the world of the segregationist practices that existed in the church. The leaders were angry, but the word had gone forth. When the 1962 meeting ended, Frank L. Peterson, an African-American became the first of his race to be elected as a vice president for the World Church. The brotherhood of man and Fatherhood of God that had stirred the 1887 meeting had not gone away.

Robert M. Kilgore, the leader from the South, had stated that if Blacks were admitted into church membership, it would be difficult to get Whites to join. When he returned home he proceeded to separate the membership of the Edgefield Junction congregation which had moved to Jefferson Street in the heart of the colored neighborhood in Nashville. He relocated the Black members to a building at 12th Street and Meharry Boulevard and sent the Whites to a new building on Natchez Trace Avenue near Vanderbilt University, stating that it was in the best interest of membership growth for the races to have separate places of worship. This position has been held by many in the church through the years, and is the opinion of some until this day. When a sizable number of Blacks join a predominately White congregation, the Whites usually move to another area or just stop attending the services on Sabbath, choosing rather to take a nature walk or engage in some other activity. In later years when Blacks started attending White churches in the North in large numbers, separate places of worship were set up for them to attend and hold membership. The same has been true for others of a different ethnic background. Until recently, it was customary for Blacks visiting a White congregation to be told where the colored church was located.

The colored young people could not understand Kilgore's move on the separation, and at least two of the Allison children left the Seventh-day Adventist Church. Florence Allison, a very talented young lady moved to Los Angeles and taught in the school system for many years but never returned to the church. Thomas went to Chicago, Illinois, and began playing in a band. When Ellen G. White learned that he had left the church, she visited with the Allison parents and urged them to go to Chicago and bring the young man back, because, she contended, the Lord had a special work for him to do. He returned and became one of the most outstanding and talented ministers of the denomination until his death in 1941.

Growth of Black membership in the church was held at bay by church leaders; however, "there is no greater force to be contended with than an idea whose time has come." The time had arrived for this people to accept the biblical teachings of God as taught by the Adventists and for them to surrender their hearts to God. African-American preachers began teaching these biblical "truths" to their people, and their membership grew by the hundreds. The numbers grew from the hundreds to the thousands. Little did the leaders of the church in 1887 realize that the Lord would bring so many people of color into the church before the end of time. By 1995, 30 percent of the membership in North America was of African descent and 90 percent of the world membership of the Seventh-day Adventist Church consisted of people of color.

Today, it seems that fear has gripped the hearts of White Seventh-day Adventists because of the change in the growth patterns of church membership in all parts of the world. From the *Daily Telegraph Newspaper* in London, England, comes this account as of March 17, 1996:

"The British Union of the Seventh-day Adventist Church (S. D. A.) is to launch a national campaign to recruit White members and plan to establish a 'Department of White Affairs'…Leaders of the S. D. A. Church believe that potential White members are daunted by predominantly black congregations…we acknowledge that race is an issue which needs to be looked at, said Pastor D. Tompkins, communication director…Many Whites have left the Church because they dislike the black style of worship with its frequent cries of 'Amen,' clapping, drums and enthusiastic singing…Whites hold 23 of the 30 seats on the Union executive committee, but the presidency is held by Jamaican-born Pastor Cecil R. Perry."

Climbing up the rough side of the mountain continues in an effort to live in heaven with the Lord.

Chapter 21

1888 And Church Upheavals In Minneapolis

*"Had Adventists after the great disappointment in 1844 held fast their faith
and followed on unitedly, in the opening providence of God...the Lord
would have wrought mightily with their effort. The work would have been
completed, and Christ would have come ere this."* Selected Messages,
Book 1, p. 68

In November 1988, Seventh-day Adventist leaders gathered in Minneapolis, Minnesota, to reflect on events that had taken place during the 100 years
from the General Conference session that was held there in 1888. At that
session, a new concept in theology was presented by Alfonso T. Jones and
Ellet J. Waggoner, two youthful editors of *The Signs of the Times* published
by the Pacific Press Publishing Association.

Jones was described by George R. Knight in his book *From 1888 to
Apostasy* as being "charismatic forceful, handsome, and tending to extremes."
He had been baptized in Walla Walla, Washington Territory, on August 8,
1874. Because of his dynamic and aggressive leadership, he soon was chosen
by the brethren to fill various posts in the church all the way to the General
Conference. The aggressive manner in which he differed with opinions and
stood his ground was not always appreciated by the leaders. Many shied away
from him. There was a rumor, circulated presumably by Willie D. White the
youngest son of James and Ellen White, that Jones was seeking to unseat James
White as president of the General Conference.

Jones and Waggoner presented thought-provoking views of justification
and righteousness by faith, which led to heated discussions fueled by misun-
derstandings, perplexity, and frustrations by some. Others expressed feelings
of gratitude for God's leading. Ellen White agreed with A. T. Jones and E. J.
Waggoner on their positions on righteousness and justification by faith and
later expressed to the leaders her conviction in the matter. She called the
message of righteousness by faith a mysterious message, to be proclaimed with
a loud voice and attended with the outpouring of His Spirit in large measure.

"The real burden of the message on righteousness by faith as presented
by them...was to affirm the truth that the only way righteousness can be
obtained is through a living faith in the lamb of God, whose blood was shed
on Calvary's cross as a propitiation for the sins of the world."—*1888–1903—
13 Crisis Years*, by A. V. Olsen, pp. 40–42.

The difference of opinion resulting from the 1888 meeting caused
division among the leaders and tended to polarize the members into two
separate bodies of Seventh-day Adventists. Jones and Waggoner continued to

hold to their beliefs and a strained relationship developed between them and the church leadership. Waggoner apostatized. Jones left the organized work and was later disfellowshipped. He never gave up the faith, as many have been led to believe.

The impact of the 1888 meeting had a profound effect on the church; its effects still linger. Many agreed with Elder Rayfield F. Warnick that the Lord was ready to close the work in 1844, 1888, and 1914, but the church was not ready. Ellen White wrote at a later time:

"It was not the will of God that the coming of Christ should be thus delayed. God did not design that His people, Israel, should wander forty years in the wilderness. He promised to lead them directly to the land of Canaan, and establish them there a holy, healthy, happy people. But those to whom it was first preached, went not in because of unbelief (Hebrews 3:19). Their hearts were filled with murmuring, rebellion, and hatred, and He could not fulfill His covenant with them.

"Had Adventists after the great disappointment in 1844 held fast their faith and followed on unitedly, in the opening providence of God, receiving the message of the third angel and in the power of the Holy Spirit proclaiming it to the world, they would have seen the salvation of God, the Lord would have wrought mightily with their effort, the work would have been completed, and Christ would have come ere this to receive His people to their reward."— *Selected Messages*, Book I, p. 68.

Despite their feuding over biblical interpretation, great emphasis was placed upon carrying the "truth" to other nations, kindred, tongues and people. For decades the leaders of the church had been carrying the work to Europe. In 1885, Stephen N. Haskel and J. O. Corliss were sent to Australia with a company of workers to open the work on this southern continent. Africa was entered two years later by D. A. Robinson, grandfather of Don Robinson, who now serves as the under treasurer of the General Conference. C. L. Boyd, Nellie Druillard and her husband joined him as they carried the message to the Solusi tribe in Rhodesia (Zimbabwe). The message was preached in Hong Kong at the same time by a layman named Abraham LaRue.

In 1899, colporteurs established the work in South America. Ellen G. White accepted a call to go overseas in 1885 to give counsel concerning the strengthening of the work in Europe. There she spent two and one half years traveling, counseling, speaking and writing. In June 1887, at Moss, Norway, she attended the first Seventh-day Adventist campmeeting held outside of the United States. Her ministry overseas helped to place the work of the church on a solid footing in Europe.

But for all its outreach efforts, the church gave no thought to sharing the truth with those in America whose roots were deep in 400 years of slavery. During the 1888 session, Charles M. Kinney introduced a proposal to the assembly that the treatment of colored people by the church should be addressed. His efforts were futile. The chairman ruled that the race question would not be discussed at that meeting. Kinney received support for his concern from A. T. Jones and John Harvey Kellogg, but little else. Kellogg and Jones had always shown themselves supportive of human rights and equality.

Very few Blacks were among the Seventh-day Adventists during this period. In fact, very few could be numbered among its entire world-wide membership. The church fathers had sent their first colored minister, C. M. Kinney, to work among the colored people in 1883. His mission later led to hundreds, thousands and millions of African descendants joining the church. They kept climbing up the rough side of the mountain in spite of adversities.

Eighteen hundred an eighty-eight should ever live in the minds of members of the Seventh-day Adventist denomination; however these members must also be mindful that there were many other historic events that were taking place during 1888. The Methodist Episcopal Church held its General Conference in New York City during this year, at which time they elected five prominent women to serve as delegates.

In 1888, a terrible blizzard took place in the eastern part of the nation that took many lives. In 1888, a group of Tennesseans fleeing Southern prejudice, settled in Topeka, Kansas, where in 1893, they founded the city's first kindergarten and "Sunday School." These were established to teach the ex-slaves to read and write. The only time that it could be done was on a Sunday, thus, the "Sunday Schools" were organized among the many religious organizations. In later years, the Seventh-day Adventists converted the concept and established "Sabbath Schools."

The year 1888 was quite a historic year of progress. The steel industry began to boom, oil companies became lucrative businesses, railroads were becoming exciting ventures, the West began to open up to settlers, the picture industry by Kodak flourished; architects began building skyscrapers in the cities, the telephone was discovered and Blacks began to play a larger role in U. S. life; Frederick Douglass became U. S. Prime minister to Haiti and spoke continually of full equality. In discussions over equality, The year 1888 was an eventful year in the annals of history.

Chapter 22

First Request For Separate Conferences

Before the Colored Methodist Episcopal Church was officially organized in 1870, five separate colored conferences existed throughout the South. So when separate Black conferences were established in the Seventh-day Adventist denomination in 1945, it was not a new thing. Such a move had been requested by Charles M. Kinney 56 years earlier.

Kinney had been ordained to the gospel ministry by the leaders of the church in 1887. He was the first African-American to have such an honor conferred upon him; however, the colored members of his congregation were not allowed to witness his ordination. They were not allowed to attend campmeetings being conducted in various places. (Campmeetings were evangelistic crusades held under a tent). These members were not allowed to attend services with White people or hold membership in White churches. It appeared that the old "Dred Scott" decision handed down by the courts of Missouri was frozen in the minds of White members—that African-Americans were only three-fifths human and really did not have a soul. In addition to this concept, ethnic bias was in the hearts of many. Coloreds were terribly mistreated by some of the White Seventh-day Adventists who at the same time were teaching about the coming of the Lord and the end of time. Segregation of the races was reaching an all time high.

In response to this rejection of his fellow members, Charles M. Kinney petitioned the denomination to establish separate conferences in the church, as had been done by the Methodist in 1870 with the birth of the Colored Methodist Episcopal Church. But his request was denied. He continued to work for racial equality in the church after the 1888 meeting in Minneapolis and requested a meeting with R. M. Kilgore, the district leader for the work in the Southern states. Kilgore had gotten the proposal for acceptance of African-Americans killed at the 1887 meeting when he said that the church would not be able to attract White people if colored people were accepted into membership.

The meeting between Kinney and Kilgore was held in Nashville, Tennessee, on October 2, 1889, to discuss colored leadership in the denomination and the establishment of colored conferences. The conversation went as follows:

Kilgore: "Now, Brother Kinney, we are ready for your statement."

C. M. Kinney

R. M. Kilgore, director of the SDA church in the South

Campmeeting in Reno, Nevada, where C. M. Kinney was encouraged to work for Colored people

Kinney meeting with church leaders in Washington, D.C.

Kinney: "It is probable that my ideas may be a little different from what has been expressed by some. But they are mere suggestions, and I would be extremely glad if there is no necessity to carry them out.

"In the first place, a separation of the colored people from White people is a great sacrifice upon our part. We lose the blessing of learning the 'truth.' I have reference especially to general meetings. The colored people as a class, are in need."

Kilgore: "What kind of separation do you refer to?"

Kinney: "I refer to the separation in the general meetings; that is, for them to have different campmeetings. No, here it would not be necessary to carry out the ideas I express. It would be a great sacrifice upon the part of my people to miss the information that these general meetings would give them; another thing, it seems to me that a separation in the general meetings would tend to destroy unity of the 'Third Angel's Message.' Now, then, this question to me is one of great embarrassment and humility, and not only to me, but to my people.

"There are four thoughts that suggest themselves to my mind that should be considered in the solution of this question: The First—is that the course that shall be taken shall be pleasing to God; The Second—that a position will be taken that will not compromise the denomination; The Third—that the position that is taken will be in the best interest of the 'cause'; Fourth—that a position will be taken that will commend itself to the good judgment of the colored people, that they may not be driven from the truth by our position on the question. Now, these are four questions that I wish to state that the 'Third Angel's Message' has the power in it to eliminate (or) remove this race prejudice upon the part of those who get hold of the 'truth.' "

Kilgore: "...That is clearly demonstrated, at least to a great extent, learned on the campground here."

Kinney: "Second, that the 'Third Angel's Message' is to go to all nations of people, that it cannot take hold of them if there is some obstacle in the way, and the 'truth' of the 'Third Angel's Message' will enable us to remove the obstacle. The 'color-line' question is an obstacle, in other words, the very existence of the colored people in church relations and other meetings is an obstacle, is a barrier that hinders the progress of the 'Third Angel's Message' from reaching many of the White people."

"Now, I wish to present twelve propositions, which, to my mind, would be a complete (or) perfect solution to the difficulty.

(1) A frank understanding between the two races on all questions affecting each. This would avoid much trouble that would otherwise occur.

(2) That colored laborers have no special desire to labor among White people, except an occasional invitation where to accept would cause no trouble.

(3) That colored brethren do not interfere with the outside interest among White people, the minister in charge of such work to be judge of such interference.

(4) Where the two races cannot meet together on religious equality, it is better to separate.

(5) That missions be established among them, thus, raising up separate churches. White laborers giving their time exclusively to this work. I realize the difficulties of White laborers, attempting to labor for both classes in the South, for if they labor for the colored people, they will lose their influence among the White people, but in laboring among the colored people exclusively that difficulty is obviated.

(6) That in view of the suicide feelings on the race question, and the hindrance it makes in accomplishing the work desired among Whites, the attendance of the colored brethren at the general meetings should not be encouraged, yet not positively forbidden. If they do attend, let there be a private, mutual understanding as to the position they should assume on every phase of the meeting.

I would say in this connection that in my judgment, a separate meeting for the colored people to be held in connection with the general meetings, (or) a clear-cut distinction, by having them occupy the back seats, etc., would not meet with as much favor from my people as a total separation. I am willing, however, to advise my people to unite with it.

(7) In those churches where there are two or more, let them remain until an effort can be made to raise up a church among them, then, have them to unite with it.

(8) Until there is enough to form a colored conference (among the colored people), the colored churches, companies (or) individuals may pay their tithes and other contributions to the regular state officers, and be considered a part of that state conference.

(9) That the General Conference do what it can in educating worthy colored laborers to engage in various branches of the work among them, when such can be found.

(10) That Christian feelings between the two races be zealously inculcated everywhere, so that the cause of reparation may not be because of the existence of prejudice within, but because of those on the outside whom you hope to reach.

(11) That when colored conferences are formed they bear the same relation to the General Conference that White conferences do.

164

(12) That these principles be applied only where this prejudice exists to the injury of the cause.

—Oakwood College Archives

Because similar racial conditions never ceased during later years, this proposal was placed before the church leaders many times thereafter. With the increase in church membership among the nonwhite groups of people in the church, positions of leadership representing these ethnic groups were sought in 1909, 1919, and 1929 to strengthen the growing work. Instead of accepting these requests, the church fathers established a Negro Department in 1909 and placed it under White leadership. The concept of White leadership was patterned after that in the Methodist Episcopal Church, which had colored conferences functioning under White leadership before the establishment of the Colored Methodist Episcopal Church. However, Bishop Othal Hawthorne Lakey in his book *The History of the CME Church* points out, "It is important to understand that the 'White brethren' as Lane refers to them, were there to advise and assist the 'colored brethren,' not to run the conference. The new church, if there were to be a new church, was to be organized by the Negro members themselves and not by the White persons in attendance."—*The History of the CME Church*, p. 37.

In Adventist circles the posture taken was that White men should be chosen as the leaders over the Black work. The practice still holds with the White union leaders presiding over the operations of the present local conferences' operations and assemblies. Church leaders seem to lean toward this posture as a guideline following a statement in Volume 9 of *Testimonies for the Church*: "Opportunities are continually presenting themselves in the Southern States, and many wise, Christian men will be called to the work. But for several reasons White men must be chosen as leaders." (9T, p. 202). This counsel was given by the prophetess when Edson was experiencing difficulties working among colored people in Mississippi. It was not for the general church; it was for that particular time and situation, although it is a church practice worldwide.

When colored leaders spoke of having their own colored-operated conferences, White leaders became enraged. J. K. Humphrey and his congregation were dismissed from the sisterhood of churches because they sought to function as a conference and to do what they believed was best for the advancement of the work among colored people. J. G. Thomas, one of the evangelists in the Southern region shared a concept of colored conferences while riding with his state president. The president stopped the car and threatened to put him out if he made the statement again. In 1929 when mention was made of colored conferences, the leaders were told to "be silent on this matter and never to mention it again until Jesus comes."

When G. E. Peters served as director of the Negro Department, he was once asked to offer a prayer and blessing over the food when the group recessed for lunch. Peters noted to his colleagues that it was interesting that "we can pray together, but we cannot eat together. I will be happy when we can get colored conferences." The chairman of the meeting, W. B. Ochs, immediately grabbed him by the collar, shook him and commanded that he "never mention such again." The impression given was that people of color had no leadership abilities, although under their leadership hundreds and thousands were being added to the church daily. The situation would reach a breaking point in 1945 as we shall discuss in later chapters.

It took some 56 years after the first request was made by Charles M. Kinney for the church fathers to agree to establish separate conferences for colored members of the Seventh-day Adventist denomination. Seven colored conferences were established and placed under colored leaders. Elder Kinney was still alive to see his request finally fulfilled. Today, some of the most productive units of the denomination are the "Regional Conferences" in the North American Division of the World Church, representing 27.08 percent of the membership in the United States and contributing 20.12 percent of the tithe for its operation; and yet, leadership positions from among this group are systematically disappearing. Inasmuch as exclusionary practices continue within the church today in the present generation, there has been many discussions concerning the establishment of regional (Black) unions to provide continued leadership for this largest minority group of people who hold membership in the church.

Chapter 23

Nashville—S. D. A. Battle Creek In The South

"Our brethren selected Nashville as a center for work in the South because the Lord in His wisdom directed them there. It is a favorable place in which to make a beginning. " Testimonies for the Church, Vol. 7, p. 232

Shortly after the Civil War ended, Northern missionary organizations went South and organized a number of schools intended to train African-American teachers, preachers and other leaders. Among these schools were Fisk University and Central Tennessee College founded in Nashville in 1866. Roger Williams University, which later became the American Baptist Theological Seminary, opened its doors in 1867.

Nashville soon became a center for the development of the African-American family. The city maintained and expanded the important community institutions established for them during slavery. Religion had been important to slaves and as historian Bobby Lee Lovett points out, it assumed new institutional functions after the emancipation. Not only was school held in the church, but the teachers were often ministers or church missionaries. The important meetings involving African-American politics, civil rights and suffrage always took place in the church. Social life also was centered around the church.

Social and fraternal organizations played important roles in the emerging African-American communities, particularly as their activities promoted group and race consciousness. In addition to creating occasions for socializing, the fraternal organizations usually provided illness or death benefits. The churches also represented African-Americans in public celebrations such as Fourth of July parades, and they served as important training grounds for African-American leaders. National orders such as the Masons, Odd Fellows, and the Good Samaritans were active throughout the South. All young men who aspired to advancement in public life sought membership in these societies, and the church was indispensable to their success.

The well-established denomination, the African Methodist Episcopal Church, organized rapidly in the South, attracting to its membership many of the more assertive young men and women of that time. Insurance companies were established; lodges, burial societies, grocery stores, cleaning establishments, laundries, day care centers for children, senior citizens' homes, orphanages and similar facilities had the church as their foundation. The doctors, the attorneys, the teachers and persons who sought to establish themselves in the town made their way to the church. Nashville was a center for these activities.

*Ellen G. White instructs that the
Lord lead the brethren to Nashville*

*Jubilee Singers from
Fisk University*

Evangelistic Crusade for Colored

*Southern Publishing Association Building
erected in Nashville*

Nashville is called the "Protestant Vatican." Publishing houses of many different denominations and other groups are found in this city. The Methodists', Baptists' and Church of Christ's publishing houses are there. Fisk University, Tennessee State University, Meharry Medical and Dental Colleges, the American Baptist Theological Seminary, all predominantly African-American institutions are located there, not to speak of many other colleges and universities. The city is a learning center in the heart of the South, also known as the "Athens of the South."

The Seventh-day Adventist denomination established a number of institutions in Battle Creek, Michigan—a hospital, a school, a publishing house and a church—but no hand was extended to the people of color who could not journey to Battle Creek for training; thus, the Lord chose Nashville as the place from which to work for this people. When the church finally turned its attention toward working for the African-American people in the South, Nashville, Tennessee, became a focal point. Ellen G. White stated in Volume 7 of *Testimonies for the Church*:

"We must provide greater facilities for the education and training of the youth, both White and Colored, in the South... Let means be gathered for the establishment of such schools. In them students may gain an education that, with God's blessing, will prepare them to win souls to Christ.

"As a people we should take a special interest in the work in Nashville. At the present time this city is a point of great importance in the Southern field. Our brethren selected Nashville as a center for work in the South because the Lord in His wisdom directed them there. It is a favorable place in which to make a beginning. Our workers will find it easier to labor in this city for the colored race than in many other cities of the South. In this city much interest is taken in the colored people by those not of our faith. In and near the city are large educational institutions for the colored people. The influence of these institutions has prepared the way for us to make this a center for our work."— *Testimonies for the Church*, Volume 7, p. 232.

Brother James Hannibal Lewis, a colored man from Battle Creek, journeyed to Nashville periodically to engage in a mission project and, while there, sought to strengthen the work among the colored people. He along with his wife, the former Luvena Cudup of Lebanon, Tennessee, worked with C. M. Kinney and organized a church in Nashville in 1894. The Nashville church became the fifth to be organized among the colored people. The Edgefield Junction church, established not far from Nashville, was the first African-American congregation in the denomination. It was originally located literally at a railroad junction stop for the Chattanooga and Nashville and the Louisville and Nashville Railroads. Still later, there were other organizations established in the surrounding areas of Franklin, Columbia, Springfield, Clarksville and Murfresboro.

Some of the families who made up the congregations in Nashville were the Jordans, the Blakes, the Allisons, the Bontempts, the Hudsons, the Hydes, the Jones, the Owens, the Wilsons, the Pattons, the Beatons, the Holders, the Freemans, the Dents, the Simons, the Brantleys, the Acklens, the Campbells, the Abbeys, the Martins, the Proctors, the Lewises and the Waltons.

Earlier, mention was made of the Allison family and of Thomas, in particular, who was chosen by God for a special ministry for Him on behalf of Black people. Thomas married Effie Margaret Ramsey, the daughter of the outstanding morticians and director of the Ramsey Funeral Home in Nashville. Mr. Ramsey was a Black financial magnet in the city whose influence was felt in many financial dealings. Mr. Zema Hill of Stevenson, Tennessee, was his close associate who later became one of the leading funeral directors in Memphis and Chattanooga. Hill was a grand uncle of Franklin Sydney Hill, II, who became a minister in the Seventh-day Adventist Church. It is whispered that when Mr. Ramsey passed away, the finance lords of Nashville brought his widow to a "crust of bread" by swallowing up all of his assets leaving her to work in service for sustenance. When Zema Hill became aware of Mrs. Ramsey's fate, he no longer placed his monies in the banking institutions but kept it in his home and on his person.

Thomas and Effie Allison had five children—Thomas, Jr., Harold, Lis, Bernard, Coteel and Clarence. Effie's first cousin, Carolyn Walton of Jackson, Tennessee, moved to Nashville to attend school and, while there, left the Spruce Street Baptist Church to become a Seventh-day Adventist. She and her husband later settled in Kansas City, Kansas, during the migrating of coloreds to the West. After settling in Kansas City, they reared and educated their children—Christine, Theresa, Ivan and Mazie. Christine became the wife of Pastor A. Gaynes Thompson, whom we mentioned in an earlier chapter.

In 1901, James Edson brought his Morning Star boat to Nashville and began to work for the people of the city. He placed his printing press in barn a on Jefferson Street in the heart of the Black community and thereafter established the Southern Publishing Association from which to print literature for poor Whites and African-American people of the South. He met with financial difficulties from time to time, but the operation continued in Nashville until it was closed in the 1980s and merged with the Review and Herald Publishing Association in Washington, D. C.

In 1902, A. G. Daniells, the president of the General Conference, along with representatives from Battle Creek visited the prophetess in her home in California with plans to close this institution, which, they stated, was in financial difficulty.

According to the *Early Elmshaven Years* by Arthur White, "The question was asked 'Shall we wait another period of time for things to evolve down there, or has the time come for the General Conference and the Southern Union

Conference men to get together and in prayerful, thoughtful counsel readjust those matters. . . and bring the business where it will not continually be going into debt?' To this Ellen White replied: 'It has; and I say, Go ahead. God's cause must not be left to reproach, no matter who is made sore by arranging matters on a right basis. Edson should give himself to the ministry and to writing, and leave alone those things that he has been forbidden by the Lord to do. Finance is not his forte at all...I do not want anyone to feel that I am sustaining Edson in a wrong. He has felt that it is terrible for me to write to him in the straight way that I have written. I have presented to him just as they are presented to me.' "—*The Elmshaven Years*, p. 191.

It seemed as if the leaders from the North took little interest in the work for this people in the South and constantly devised ways to shut it down.

Elder Daniells left California that night with a copy of the interview. The Lord spoke to Ellen White in vision concerning the matter and command that the place should never be closed but that it should stand to spread the message like leaves of autumn across the South.

"On Monday, within twenty-four hours of the interview that was held at Elmshaven, Ellen White wrote a letter addressed to 'Dear Brethren':

"Last night I seemed to be in the operating room of a large hospital, to which people were being brought, and instruments were being prepared to cut off their limbs in a big hurry...One came in who seemed to have authority, and said to the physicians, 'Is it necessary to bring these people into this room?' Looking pityingly at the sufferer, he said, 'Never amputate a limb until everything possible has been done to restore it.' Examining the limbs which the physicians had been preparing to cut off, he said, 'They may be saved, the first work is to use every available means to restore these limbs.'

"What a fearful mistake it would be to amputate a limb that could be saved by patient care. Your conclusions have been too hastily drawn. Put these patients in the best rooms in the hospital, and give them the very best care and treatment. Use every means in your power to save them from going through life in a crippled condition, their usefulness damaged for life.

"The sufferers were removed to a pleasant room, and faithful helpers cared for them under the speaker's direction, and not a limb had to be sacrificed."—Letter 162, 1902. *The Elmshaven Years*, pp. 191, 192.

The leaders from Battle Creek were disappointed, the Southern Publishing House was spared until 1980. With the closing of this house, Seventh-day Adventists surrendered the publishing base in the South, and truth-filled literature from this organization ceased to flow; whereas publishing plants of other organization still serve their people throughout the South and the world with their Nashville operations.

Nashville was designated by God to be a base from which to work for the people of the South. It was to serve in this area as Battle Creek served its purpose in the North. At the turn of the century, Dr. Lottie Isabel along with Zelda Challen traveled to Nashville and established the Rock Creek Sanitarium on Cherry Street, but it was soon closed and Dr. Isabel joined the teaching staff at the Meharry School of medicine. In later years Nellie Druillard opened the Riverside Sanitarium for coloreds in Nashville; it also was closed in 1980. The Hillcrest School for colored children was opened on Whites Creek Pike in Nashville at the turn of the century, and it was closed.

The city is a center established by God for the purpose of spreading the gospel of Jesus Christ throughout the South and to the ends of the earth. Some leaders sought to hinder the work among people of African heritage in the South and in a number of instances closed up the work among this people. But the Lord is still with this people, and many talents found among them will continue to be used to the glory of God as they continue to climb up the rough side of the mountain while on their way to enjoy the promised land.

J. EDSON WHITES' MISSION IN THE SOUTH

J. Edson White

Edson talking to Cynthia Johnson in front of the Morning Star Boat in Bicksburg, Mississippi (she is the mother of Garland Millet)

Vicksburg National Military Park

Elder Frank L. Bland and Miss E. Irvin discuss the boat docking in front of her father's lumber business in Vicksburg.

Large tent in which evangelistic meetings were held in on the hillside of Vicksburg.

T. H. Buckner returned home from St. Louis to promote the work of the church

Chapter 24

James Edson White's Mission To Colored Americans

"Eternity alone will reveal the work accomplished for the colored people by the small schools at Vicksburg, Yazoo City and other points in the South. In this field we need many more such schools." Testimonies for the Church, Vol. 7, p. 231

James Edson White, the second son of the prophetess Ellen G. White and James E. White, felt impressed to work for the colored people of the South after he restored his relationship with the Lord in 1893. With some difficulty, he eventually located some pamphlets his mother had written concerning the church's duty to the colored people of the South and set about to follow the visions she had spoken of in those pamphlets.

With the help of Will O. Palmer, James Edson built a boat on the banks of the Kalamazoo River in Allegan, Michigan, the hometown of M. D. Gordon, president of the Southern Union Conference in the North American Division. He would use the boat on the river as a church from which to preach, a school from which to teach and as a house in which to live while on his mission to help these downtrodden people.

He received very little, if any, encouragement from the leaders at Battle Creek. In fact, Uriah Smith, the editor of the *Review and Herald* church paper, had told him that his mother had never written anything concerning these people in the South. The janitor shared information with him to the contrary and related that he had been given instructions just moments before to discard some information concerning this work. Edson retrieved the works from the trash heap and combined the pamphlets to produce a book entitled *The Southern Work*.

Money was scarce, and he had to sell his publications to finance the journey. After reaching his destination, his mother pleaded with the leaders of the church to help Edson with this venture. The membership responded by giving liberally, but the money was kept by the brethren and applied to supposed obligations that had been made with the Review and Herald Publishing Company in Battle Creek.

Edson finally reached Vicksburg and was able to secure a place to dock his boat in front of Irvins' lumberyard. Mr. Irvin was an African-American with a thriving lumber business in Vicksburg and had customers for miles around. He proved to be a blessing to this missionary who had come from the North to help his people. Later on, the Irvin family became members of the church after listening to the teachings of Edson White. White used Vicksburg as a base for his operation but traveled throughout central Mississippi and up and down the Mississippi, Yazoo and Cumberland Rivers bringing help to former slaves and their children who lived in these parts. Madlyn Edwards of Vicksburg attended the school on the Morning Star boat between the years of 1895 and 1901. She recalled being the "cutest thing on the boat" in those days as she reflected on some of the events that transpired and the people who lived there at the time.

Vicksburg is located on the Mississippi River halfway between Memphis, Tennessee, and New Orleans, Louisiana. It was historically famous as the site of one of the most decisive campaigns of the American Civil War. It owes its importance in peace and war to its geographical location, for it was here in 1719 the Frenchmen built Fort St. Pierre and began commercial activity for many of the settlers. By 1825, it had become a lusty frontier river town warring with gamblers and claiming the lives of five heroic and individualist newspaper editors by violence over a period of 22 years. It was rough territory.

During the Civil War, this city became another key point of fighting in 1862 and 1863. It was here that General U. S. Grant and his troops broke the back of resistance and brought the war to an end. Thousands of soldiers from the North and the South died in combat and were buried in the National Cemetery. A tour through the National Park shows the distinct sections where these men were buried, a section where the North buried its dead and a section where the South buried its dead.

When Grant arrived there, he burned the town to the ground, as had been done in many other cities throughout the South, but he decided that Port Gibson, located about 26 miles south of Vicksburg, was too beautiful to be burned.

Three decades after the war had ended, racial problems still existed in Vicksburg. Not only were White people prejudiced against people of other races, but racial overtones existed among African-Americans. Friction between light-skinned and dark-skinned people persisted, not only in Vicksburg but throughout the land.

As a result of Edson White's preaching and teaching, many gladly heard and accepted his teachings. Some of those in Vicksburg who became adherents were Thomas Kelly, the town barber, who later became a Seventh-day Adventist preacher; Maggie Shoup, whose daughter still lives in Vicksburg; Etta Littlejohn, the mother of Charles E. Bradford, the only African-American to serve as the president of the North American Division of the World Church of Seventh-day Adventists (she became a nurse and attended Ellen White when she was a patient at the New England Sanitarium); Cynthia Johnson, the mother of Garland J. Millett, former president of Oakwood College; and the mother of the Edmond Family whose children James and Lorraine became faithful leaders in the church in Cleveland, Ohio.

*Madlyn Edwards of Vicksburg discusses days when she
was a student on the boat in 1896*

*General Conference President R. H. Pierson standing by the Yazoo City,
Mississippi church building and listens to the stories of the work
as told by the pioneer's children.*

*Church and
school
buildings
erected by
Edson
throughout
the state*

*The origi-
nal school
building in
Yazoo City
in which
Naomi
Warnick
taught in
the 1800s*

The Morning Star boat that sailed from Michigan to Mississippi

OTHER CITIES IN MISSISSIPPI WHERE WORK WAS BEGUN

Natchez, Mississippi

*The late Mrs.
M. Johnson*

*Richard Wright,
playwright*

*The late Walter Jones of Clarksdale and the late Robert Seard of
Greenville were pioneers of the churches in Mississippi*

*The late Leon Peterson of Meridian, a classmate of James Weldon
Johnson, was another pioneer of the church in Mississippi*

*The Lewis Frazier family of Montgomery, Alabama
were converts of T. B. Buckner of Vicksburg*

A street in the little town of Edwards, Mississippi, has been named "Morning Star," in remembrance and appreciation for the work done by Edson White and his people on behalf of the colored people of Mississippi. Edson went up and down the rivers and streams and from place to place setting up schools and constructing church buildings for the people. He would build some prefabricated buildings at his base of operation in Vicksburg and carry them to other towns and villages and assemble them for the people. One such building still remains in Yazoo City—the Lintonia Chapel, and a school still stands in Natchez. Sister A. Johnson attended the school. She was the last of the charter members of the church in Natchez when she passed away in 1991. Other persons who were also members of the Natchez church were: Dr. Ruth Temple who graduated from the College of Medical Evangelists in Loma Linda, California. She had been brought to Natchez by her Baptist parents who came as members of the American Missionary Society in Ohio. The mother of Carl A. Dent who later served as a teacher at the Huntsville school in Alabama was also a member of the church in Mississippi when Carl and his sister were very young children. She had come to Natchez with her husband to serve with the American Missionary Society. Her husband is buried in Natchez. Another member of the church was the mother of Richard Wright, the playwright. Richard wrote the books, *Raisin In the Sun* and *Black Boy*. He lived at the Huntsville school at one time.

Madlyn Edwards recalls the day the boat docked and children began to attend the floating school in Vicksburg. She was but a small child but remembers her grandmother Maggie Shoup and her mother Margaret Maxie joining the Seventh-day Adventist Church under the teachings of Edson White. Her sisters, Lillian and Laura also attended the school.

Not only did this school serve the needs of the people of Vicksburg, but when it was told that Edson's mission really was for the benefit of colored children in the South, students came from far and near. Some came from across the river in Louisiana; some from as far away as Memphis, Tennessee. Many were educated at the school, including Harry Gray, son of Ella Gray of Memphis, Tennessee, who became the president of the Musicians' Guild in Chicago; Frank L. Bland of Newelton, Louisiana, in later years attended the school at Vicksburg. He became a pastor, evangelist, and one of the vice-presidents for the World Church. Thomas Murphy also attended the school and became a minister, and Etta Littlejohn attended and later married Robert L. Bradford, a minister for the church.

Racial tensions continued, and African-Americans and their White teachers from the North became known as "trouble makers." The Black preachers who were losing members to this "Saturday church-going group" stirred up the Whites by telling falsehoods about the group; besides, when the people began attending church on Saturday the plantation owners were losing workers in the field on that day. This led to problems. Edson wrote his mother reporting an incident that took place in May 14,1899. This was the account as written by Ron Graybill in his book *E. G. White and Church Race Relations*:

"Two weeks ago tonight a mob of about 25 White men came to our church at Calmer at about midnight. They brought out Brother Stephenson, our worker, and then hunted for Brother Casey, our leading colored brother of that place, but he had escaped in time so they did not reach him. They then went to the house of Brother Olvin, called him out, and whipped him with a cowhide. I think they would have killed him if it had not been for a friendly White man who ordered them to stop whipping after they had struck a few blows. They did not pay any attention to him at first, but he drew his revolver, and said the next man who struck a blow would hear from him, and then they stopped. During the time they shot at Brother Olvin's wife, and struck her in the leg, but did not hurt her seriously. They took Brother Stephenson to the nearest railway station, put him on the cars, and sent him out of the state. They posted notice on the church forbidding me to return, and forbidding the steamer Morning Star to land between Yazoo City and Vicksburg.

"The whole difficulty arose from our efforts to aid the colored people. We had given them clothing where in need, and food to those who were hungry, and had taught them some better ideas about farming, introduced different seeds such as peanuts, beans, etc., that bring a high price…and this the Whites would not stand."—*E. G. White and Church Race Relations*, pp. 56, 57.

When Edson related the experience to his mother, the prophetess instructed him not to place the coloreds on equality with the Whites in that community and that setting because of the life-threatening conditions that existed. Regretfully, her statement was taken out of context by church leaders who made it a standard policy for race relations in the church everywhere. Segregation within the church became the accepted procedure in many places. Her admonition for that specific situation had been:

"The colored people should not urge that they be placed on an equality with White people. The relation of the two races has been a matter hard to deal with, and I fear that it will ever remain a most perplexing problem. So far as possible, everything that would stir up the race prejudice of the White people should be avoided. There is danger of closing the door so that our White laborers will not be able to work in some places in the South…

"The work of proclaiming the truth for this time is not to be hindered by an effort to adjust the position of the Negro race…If we move quietly and judiciously, laboring in the way that God has marked out, both White and colored people will be benefited by our labors."—*Testimonies for the Church*, Vol. 9, p. 214.

On one occasion when Ellen White was on her way to visit the work in Vicksburg, a colored minister named Frank Warnick was traveling with her on the train. Without explanation, she instructed him to leave the train at

Redwood, about 15 miles from Vicksburg. Warnick, a very fair skinned man, followed the instructions and later learned that a mob was waiting at the station in Vicksburg to lynch him. The mob thought that Warnick was trying to pass himself off as a White man. At another time, when T. B. Buckner, was traveling on a train in the "Jim Crow" car he was ordered to leave that section and get "up front where you belong." Buckner's response was: "You White folk have messed us up so until you don't know who we are!"

Such were the conditions under which Edson White labored for the colored people. He was able to get a few of the leaders of the church such as Will O. Palmer and Louis A. Hansen to join him in the South. Colored members from the North came to help spread the gospel among the people. Some who came from New Jersey and Delaware could easily have been mistaken as being of the White race.

Colored people were encouraged to work for their own people, and this they did. As a result, the work began to grow throughout the Southland, especially in the state of Mississippi. Mrs. White had said:

"Instead of wondering whether they are not fitted to labor for White people, let our colored brethren and sisters devote themselves to missionary work among the colored people. There is an abundance of room for intelligent colored men and women to labor for their own people. Much work remains to be done in the Southern field. Special efforts are to be made in the large cities. In each of these cities there are thousands of colored people, to whom the last warning message of mercy must be given. Let the missionary spirit be awakened in the hearts of our colored members. Let earnest work be done for those who know not the truth."—*Testimonies for the Church*, Vol. 9, p. 199. This statement also was taken out of context and made a blanket policy for the entire church.

Elder Frank Warnick, the preacher and possibly distant relative of Edson White, had already responded to the call to help with the work Edson had begun in Mississippi. His daughter, Naomi, also joined him in the mission and served as a teacher for the school in Yazoo City. Elder John F. Street, another distant relative, came from Delaware to help in the Delta of Mississippi, Greenville and Clarksdale. In later years, Brother Robert Seard of Greenville and Brother Walter Jones of Clarksdale became strong supporters of these men who had come to work for their people. Brother Seard had moved from Memphis, Tennessee, to Greenville to help with the work and was later asked to serve as a pastor for the church, but he refused because he felt that he could better serve witnessing as a layman while continuing his house moving business. Brother Jones, a native of Clarksdale, used his influence to spread the gospel through his area and surrounding territories operating his 40-acre farm and his local taxi business. In Greenwood, Mississippi, 50 miles east of Greenville, Sisters I. Dickerson, Alyce Scales and C. Scruggs came from New Orleans to help stabilize the work in the heart of the delta.

Elder Tazwell B. Buckner was living in St. Louis, Missouri, as a White man when he learned of the Seventh-day Adventist's teachings through the preaching of J. N. Loughborough and became a member of the church. When C. M. Kinney was sent to organize the work among the people in Louisville, Kentucky, Buckner was placed in charge of the work in St. Louis. Under conviction by the Holy Spirit, he later returned to his hometown of Vicksburg to work for his own people.

"W. G. Buckner, a prosperous White Seventh-day Adventist, had erected a large building on Early Street in Montgomery, which he called the Charity Mission. Seeing Tazwell B. Buckner's name in reports to the union paper and assuming he was a distant relative, W. G. Buckner invited T. B. Buckner to Montgomery to assist with the founding of a church and church school. Within a few months the two Buckner families had organized a church school and in the spring of 1899 a congregation consisting of the Fountain, Johnson and Fraziers families."—*We Have Tomorrow*, p. 122.

A congregation was also established just 50 miles to the west of Montgomery in Selma. T. B. Buckner later was sent to oversee the work in Orleans, Louisiana, and finally to Detroit where he spent his last days ministering to his people.

Although blind for 50 years, Leon Peterson of Meridian became a dedicated lay worker of the church among the people of that city. One of nine children born to Adam Craig and Annie Peterson, Leon attended the Baptist Seminary, the Wesley and Lincoln Schools in Meridian and began studying for the ministry. He left the community to study science and biology when he decided to become a physician. His advance studies took him to Howard and Columbia Universities where he became a schoolmate of James Weldon Johnson, author of the Negro National Anthem. After living away from his hometown for almost 20 years, Peterson was told that his parents, along with Robert and Mary Emerson and Albert Johnson and his wife, had embraced a new doctrine about Sabbathkeeping that was being taught by a Brutus Howard Ewing of nearby Okalona, Mississippi.

Peterson immediately returned home to help straighten out his parents' thinking, only to embrace the teaching himself. Unfortunately, his eyesight began to fail, and he finally became completely blind. However, this did not deter him; he became a determined and strong leader of the church in Meridian and throughout the state.

Theodore Troy and his wife of Oberlin, Ohio, responded to the request to teach in Mississippi among the downtrodden people whose roots were in slavery. They joined the American Missionary Society and went to Tugaloo, Mississippi, to teach at Tugaloo School in nearby Jackson before settling in California to develop the work among coloreds there.

Miss Anna Knight of Soso, Mississippi, served as a missionary in India for 16 years. She became burdened for her people and returned home to serve as a teacher and church leader. Ofttimes she would tell her experience of having to keep a shot gun in the corner of her school room to discourage the "would-be" trouble makers who were opposed to the education of colored people in that part of Mississippi. In later years she became the superintendent of schools in the Southern Union, a post she held until retirement.

Finis Parker, the pilot of Edson's boat spent his last days in Yazoo City. He was from Logansport, Indiana, and a relative of the Fords, Humphreys and Hurts whose next generation of children became dedicated workers for the denomination.

When Edson began his work in Columbus, Amory and West Point, Mississippi, some families who responded to the teachings were the parents of Harry and Queen Ester Davis of Memphis, Tennessee, the Mitchells of Detroit, Michigan, the Lees of Huntsville, Alabama, and the Blanchards of Chicago, Illinois.

These leaders and others were among the colored people in the state of Mississippi who responded to Ellen White's pleas not to neglect "our duty to the colored people" and worked to help bring the gospel to their own people.

Edson White's wife Emma had faithfully stood by his side during his mission to colored America in Mississippi. Her health began to fail, leading the family to seek another base from which to operate. They subsequently took the mission boat to Nashville, Tennessee.

Once in Nashville, Edson established a printing operation to publish the "truth" of God's word. This venture marked the beginning of the Southern Publishing Association. Before the Morning Star caught fire and burned on the Cumberland River, just 20 miles north of Nashville, Edson returned to Battle Creek where he died and was buried. He had established more than 50 schools for the colored people. The star from the boat was taken to the school for workers' children in Huntsville, the boiler was later placed at Nellie Druillard's Riverside Sanitarium for colored people, and the little bell used to call the Sabbath School to order in Yazoo City is still being used by the people there. The large bell from the boat was left at Vicksburg but has since been transferred to the Archives Room at Oakwood College.

Edson engaged in many exploits to bring the message to the colored people of the South. The work that was begun in the Southland has spread across the United States and around the world. His mission boat, The Morning Star, was really guided by God Himself and served as a memorial of how the Lord used this "black sheep of the White family" to share the gospel with all of God's children throughout the Southland.

Ellen White constantly shared her concerns for her son's mission and had a burden that the work not cease when others who did not have the same vision took over the reins of leadership of the church. She, therefore, made provisions in her Last Will and Testament for the support of the project. Before she passed away, she made this provision for the continued advancement of the work among the colored people of America. Her will reads thus:

(a) To pay my son, James Edson White, annually during his natural life ten (10) percent of the net proceeds of said properties for his sole life and use and benefit, and upon his death to Emma L. White, his wife, during her natural life should she survive him...

2. If the entire remainder of said net proceeds from my said properties is more than sufficient to pay, with interest, in the manner in which my creditors shall agree to receive payments of their respective claims, then my said trustees shall use the overplus for the improvement of the books and manuscripts held in trust by them, and herein provided; for securing and printing a new translation thereof, missionary work of the Seventh-day Adventist denomination, for the support of mission schools, under the Negro Department of the Seventh-day Adventist General Conference for the support of mission schools for illiterate whites in the Southern states. Provided, however, that said trustees are hereby empowered and directed to sell my said real property of so much thereof as may be necessary to pay the following sums...

SIXTH: "After the death of James Edson White and his wife, my said trustees are hereby empowered and directed to apply the amount prescribed in subdivision (a) paragraph FIFTH toward the discharge of any legal claims against the estate of said James Edson White, shall be applied to the maintenance of the mission schools for Negroes now conducted by the Negro Department of the Seventh-day Adventist General Conference."—*Ellen G. White and Her Critics*, pp. 676, 677.

In later years, when questioned about the execution of Ellen G. White's will concerning the monies from the sale of her millions of books and manuscripts, the trustees' response to these probing leaders of the Black work was that the will was "dry" and had no relevance. When inquiries were made of White Southern attorneys concerning the meaning of a "dry" will, they were told that there is no such thing as a "dry" will. Further investigations into the "dry" will theory could prove to be interesting.

Regardless of the charges and counter charges that have been made concerning this Last Will and Testament, it is evident that the Lord used James Edson White to carry the message of hope to the colored people of the South, and the rippling effects of his mission will be felt around the world until the end of time as Black people continue climbing up the rough side of the mountain to reach their heavenly home.

Chapter 25

Huntsville Training School For Colored Youth

"Instruction was given me that this farm must not be sold; that the situation possesses many advantages for the carrying forward of a colored school. It would take years to build up in a new place the work that has been done in Huntsville." The Huntsville School,(a tract) pp. 9, 10

Many schools established for training of African-American students were found in the South. The Catholic church was quietly moving among this people training them to be leaders by establishing schools such as Xavier in New Orleans, Louisiana; St. Jude in Montgomery, Alabama; St. Charles in Chicago, Illinois; and St. Benedict, among others. The American Missionary Societies from the North had established Fisk University, Daniel Paine College, Knoxville College, LeMoyne College, Tugaloo College, Hampton Institute and Rust College. The governments also began establishing state supported schools such as Tuskegee Institute, A. & T. College, A. & M. College, Howard University, Kentucky State University and others.

The Seventh-day Adventist Church was among the last denominations to establish schools for training descendants of former slaves. After plans for a school were laid, the 360-acre site in Huntsville, Alabama, purchased and some objections overcome, the school opened its doors in 1896 with an enrollment of 16 students from Tennessee, Mississippi and Alabama. They were Frank Brice, George Graham, Etta Grimes, Robert Hancock, Etta Littlejohn, Mary McBee, Naomi McNeal, Charles Morford, Mary Morford, Thomas Murphy, Lela Peck, Daisy Pollard, Grant Royston, Samuel J. Thompson and Frances Worthington. Few were members of the Adventist church.

In 1896 when the Huntsville Training School was established, Ole A. Olsen, a Norwegian, was the president of the General Conference. Succeeding him in 1897 was George A. Irwin, who served as the director of the Adventist work in the South and was particularly interested in helping African-Americans adapt to life in the mainstream of society. C. M. Kinney had found the site and recommended it to the leaders as a place to start a school. One of the first buildings to be erected was a girls' dormitory named Irwin Hall. The Old Mansion that had served as an auction place for slaves became the living quarters for the staff and room for instructing the students. The boys lived in tents and shanties that had served as slaves quarters before the war. On more than one occasion the two sons of Pastor Alonzo Barry of Louisville, who were students, burned the outside toilets to the ground. They were immediately restored; the boys were dismissed.

BEGINNING DAYS AT THE HUNTSVILLE SCHOOL

C. M. Kinney

Solon M. Jacobs

*The Old Mansion where President Andrew Jackson
frequently visited*

*Grandpa Haywood
Moore, a former slave
on the plantation*

Faculty members at the school during the early years.

SOME OF THE FIRST 16 STUDENTS TO ENTER THE HUNTSVILLE SCHOOL IN 1896

Samuel J. Thompson, foster son of the Allison family in Clarksville, Tennessee

Mary (McBee) Thompson of Knoxville, TN (After their marriage they settled in Knoxville)

Etta (Littlejohn) Bradford of Vicksburg, Mississippi

Another student, not pictured, was Frances (Worhtington) Campbell Lynch of Clinton Tennessee

Oliver McKinney, whose father was in the second class to enter the school in 1897.

T. B. Buckner, first Colored member to serve on the school board

The Administration Building

SCHOOL LEADERS MAINTAINED A
'TRAIN THE HAND' CONCEPT

Students were awakened daily with the ringing of the bell in the front of Old Mansion which had been used for slaves to begin their daily chores

Ladies were taught sewing

Men were taught farming

Cotton grown on the farm was carried to Huntsville to be sold

The first principal of the school was Solon M. Jacobs; he was followed by H. S. Shaw, C. J. Boyd and J. L. Tucker. All of these men were White and operated from the concept that African-Americans should be taught chiefly to farm, work railroad beds and perform domestic chores. This was the thinking prevalent in the South at the time, but students desired to be trained for leadership positions that would equip them to take the gospel message to their fellow brothers and sisters in their communities back home. The teachers sought to follow the Booker T. Washington philosophy of training the hands; the students espoused the W. E. B. Dubois philosophy of training the mind. However, the blueprint for education that the Lord had instructed Ellen White to follow involved the training of the heart, head and hand.

This difference in philosophies brought restlessness among the student body from time to time over the years. The students demanded that more colored teachers be added to the staff, but their concerns were not addressed until those of following generations moved to get the situation changed. By 1899, changes were made in the curriculum, and two-year diplomas were awarded for completion of what was termed "the common branches," with emphasis placed on agriculture, carpentry, blacksmithing and other industries.

N. E. Ashby, one of the early students who later became a faculty member, related an experience of students sitting on the campus one Sabbath afternoon singing the song "I'm going to tell God how you treat me one of these days." With tears in his eyes, one of the teachers approached them and inquired, "What have we done to you?" This was the kind of misunderstanding that existed between faculty and students in the early days of the school.

By 1902, leaders of the church, under President A. G. Daniells, felt that the school project was a financial drain on the denomination; so they moved to close the school. But their effort to do so were unsuccessful.

When Ellen White visited the campus in 1904, however, she stated that that was the very spot that the Lord had shown to her in vision, and she insisted that not one acre of it be sold. By this time, the church was not supporting the school in a way that would make it successful. S. M. Jacobs and his wife were paying dearly for their service. A lack of interest among the leaders left them to bear full responsibility, which almost cost them their health. About this situation, Ellen G. White wrote:

"Brother Jacobs put forth most earnest, disinterested efforts, but he was not given the help that his strength demanded. Sister Jacobs also worked too hard, and when her health began to give way, they decided to leave Huntsville and go to some place where the strain would not be so heavy. Had they then been furnished with efficient helpers, and with means to make the needed improvement, it would have given courage to Brother Jacobs, to the students, and to our people everywhere. But the means that ought to have gone to

Huntsville did not go, and we see the result in the present showing."—*Review and Herald*, September 1, 1904.

Money had been sent from Ohio to support the school, but it was not accounted for. When T. B. Buckner, the first colored to serve on the board of directors, brought the leaders into question concerning the disappearance of this money, he was dismissed from the work. However, he earned more working outside of the organized work than he did working for the church. He was asked to return to the ministry but decided against it.

Regarding sale of the Huntsville property, Mrs. White further wrote: "Recently the question was asked me, 'Would it not be well to sell the school land at Huntsville, and buy a smaller place?' Instruction was given me that this farm must not be sold; that the situation poses many advantages for the carrying forward of a colored school. It would take years to build up in a new place the work that has been done in Huntsville."

"In order that the school may advance as it should, money is needed, and sound intelligent generalship. Things are to be well kept up, and the school is to give evidence that Seventh-day Adventists mean to make a success of whatever they undertake.

"The facilities necessary for the success of the school must be provided. At the present the facilities are very meager. A small building should be put up, in which the students can be taught how to care for one another in times of sickness. There has been a nurse at the school to look after the students when they were sick, but no facilities have been provided. This has made the work very discouraging.

"The students are to be given a training in those lines of work that will help them to be successful laborers for Christ…The man who takes charge of the Huntsville school should know how to govern himself and how to govern others. The Bible teacher should be a man who can teach the students how to present the truths of the Word of God in public, and how to do house-to-house work. The business affairs of the farm are to be wisely and carefully managed.

"The teachers should constantly seek wisdom from on high, that they may be kept from making mistakes. They should give careful attention to their work, that each student may be prepared for the line of service to which he is better adapted. All are to be prepared to serve faithfully in some capacity. Teachers and students are to cooperate in doing their best. The constant effort of the teachers should be to make the student see the importance of constantly rising higher and still higher.

"The leading, controlling influence in the school is to be faithfulness in that which is least. Thus students will be prepared to be faithful in greater things. Each student is to take himself in hand, and with God's help overcome the faults that mar his character."—*Review and Herald*, September 1, 1904.

Some students attending at this time were John Green from Shreveport, Louisiana; Mary Butler from Palatka, Florida; Joseph H. Laurence from St. Kitts in what was then the British West Indies; Eva Deloney from Tuscumbia, Alabama; and C. Henri who came from Trinidad, also in the British West Indies. In an effort to prepare themselves for service to mankind, they had come to this school established by God to help them with their preparations. They were climbing up the rough side of the mountain to achieve their goals, and they would make it.

Chapter 26

Training Blacks To Be Medical Evangelists

Along with a distinct belief in Sabbath observance and the literal return of Christ to earth again, the Seventh-day Adventist denomination has proclaimed the importance of health and healing to the Christian life. Belief in sound principles of health has helped to make the members of this denomination a distinct people in all parts of the world.

A New England farmer, while smoking and contemplating the return of his Lord, suddenly questioned whether he wanted Jesus to see him with a pipe in his mouth? He buried the pipe along with his tobacco pouch in a furrow and told the story at prayer meeting that evening. The story spread far and wide, and by the fall of 1844 many Adventists had discontinued the use of tobacco in all of its forms. In the December 1853 issue of the *Review and Herald*, the first article appeared denouncing the use of tobacco in any of its forms, and in 1855 its use became a test of church membership. Later, members began to promote vegetarianism and to abstain from using pork, tea, coffee, and other irritating foods, which the surgeon general of the United States in recent years has confirmed are injurious to health. A television news account of November 9, 1993, stated that more people die from the use of tobacco than from any other cause of death.

Incidentally, before World War II Adolph Hitler made public his intentions of building what would be known as a "master race" of people. He became a vegetarian and influenced some of his followers to follow the same health practices. He had learned about health principles by reading Seventh-day Adventist books owned by his step mother, who was a member of the church.

In 1866, Ellen G. White encouraged the dissemination of health information, saying that this work was not to depend upon the pulpit alone. She urged the establishment of institutions from which these teachings could be enlarged upon. In May 1866, the eight acre farm of Judge Graves was bought just outside of Battle Creek, Michigan, and in September of the same year, the Western Health Reform Institute was established by the Seventh-day Adventist Church.

John Harvey Kellogg, the brother of W. K. Kellogg of breakfast cereal fame, became the director of the institute in 1874. He later changed the name to the Battle Creek Sanitarium and established the American Missionary College in connection with it. The medical arm of the church's ministry came to be known as the "right arm" of its teachings.

In 1896, the denomination established the International Medical Missionary and Benevolent Association and invited African-Americans and other groups to be trained. Kellogg opened the doors at Battle Creek to all men and women who were ready to devote their lives to Christian service. Kellogg used the *Review and Herald*, whose headquarters was then also located in Battle Creek, to get the word out. Each week he sent bundles of papers down to the docks to be placed on ships with instructions to the crews to drop them off at the ports where they stopped. Responses came from all parts of the globe, including the West Indies, Africa, India, Bermuda, South America and Southern United States.

Many prominent African-American physicians and nurses received training at the International Medical Missionary and Benevolent Association between the years of 1896 and 1917. These medical missionaries learned from Dr. Kellogg the basic concepts of the healing arts, hydrotherapy, physiotherapy, diets and foods and general health principles as set forth in the writings of the Spirit of Prophecy.

Dr. Kellogg boldly opened the doors at Battle Creek to some 67 Black students who entered to learn and departed to serve mankind. But by 1906, the church leaders had withdrawn their support from the school and in 1910 opened another school in Loma Linda, California, to train its medical evangelists. However, 35 of those Blacks who received their training at Battle Creek dedicated themselves to doing medical evangelism for the church. According to the book *Angels in Ebony* by Jacob Justiss, several of them, including Irene Jackson, William Price, Mary Dugood, Grace Guy, Lula Seacy, Mary Holt and Ned Graves, stayed at the sanitarium in Battle Creek to work. Robert Jefferson, a male nurse, served A. T. Jones, one of the leaders of the 1888 Movement and President Warren G. Harding.[1]

"Those students who entered foreign mission service at the behest of the General Conference included Prince Mark Njoi of the Congo (Zaire), Dr. Simmie who returned to his homeland of French Guiana to serve his people and Philip Giddings and his wife who went to Haiti to serve as doctor and nurse. Dr. and Mrs. Morrell served on the African continent, Anna Knight worked in India, Dr. Lottie Blake and Dr. D. E. Blake did self-supporting work in Panama; Doris Skeeret and husband Elder C. H. Cave served in Barbados and Mr. Reid returned to Bermuda and worked there.

---

1   Harding's mother was a Seventh-day Adventist; his sister, Carolyn Pheeby Volau also a member of the church, served as a missionary to Burma. Harding was said to be of Negro heritage. During a visit in Birmingham, Alabama, where he spoke before a gathering of Whites and Blacks, he raised his voice against segregation and racism.

LEADERS IN THE MEDICAL FIELD

Dr. John Harvey Kellogg courageously opened the doors at Battle Creek to some 67 Black students who entered to learn and departed to serve mankind

Judge and Mrs. James Price of Birmingham, founders of Birmingham Institute

Mrs. Zelda (Challen) Willis, graduate nurse of the school

Dr. Lottie (Isabel) Blake, Battle Creek graduate, established the Rock City Sanitarium in Nashville and later served as an instructor at Meharry Medical College

Dr. Grace Kimbrough established a medical practice in Philadelphia

First Oakwood graduating class of nurses. Photo taken August, 1908

"And there were also those who chose the Southland in America to labor for the people, but had to endure some very trying circumstances. Some of these were: (1) Louise Bodie; (2) James Price Pearson, born a slave, but after the Emancipation Proclamation became a county judge in Birmingham, Alabama, during the reconstruction days. After receiving his training, Judge Pearson returned home to establish the Birmingham Institute in Sterrett, Alabama. He established a treatment room in one of the department stores in downtown Birmingham where he served the White people during the day and the Black people in the evening after hours. Daisy Pollard and Elizabeth Wright started a school in Denmark, South Carolina, which later became The Vorhees Junior College operated by the Episcopal Church. Jesse Dorsey became the wife of Attorney W. H. Green, first to serve as the director of the Colored Department of the General Conference in 1918. Jesse went to LaMonte Hunter School in Kentucky. Georgia Sebastian became the wife of Elder Sebastian, one of the early pioneers of the church…Emma Taylor married Frank G. Warnick, a minister who worked with James Edson White throughout the state of Mississippi…Mamie Isabel worked as a nurse in Nashville, Tennessee, along with Zelda Challen."—*Angels in Ebony*, pp. 94–96.

Other schools were established to train African-Americans in the fields of medicine and dentistry and other allied health disciplines. Howard University, named after General Otis Howard who headed the postwar Freedman's Bureau was chartered in Washington, D. C., opened its doors in 1867 to many of our youth who pursued the health fields. The first successful heart surgery was performed over 100 years ago by Dr. Daniel Hale Williams, a product of Howard University.

The Meharry Medical/Dental College was founded in 1876 as a department of the Central Tennessee University of Nashville. The department became an independent college in 1915 and graduated thousands of Black youth who through the years have served on missions of mercy to their people and mankind. Dr. D. E. Blake, the husband of Dr. Lottie Blake was the first Seventh-day Adventist to graduate from the school of medicine.

As Jesus went through the land bringing help to the suffering and dying, these medical evangelist of the church administered to the needs of mankind physically, mentally and spiritually. It must be said, however, that they were medical evangelists who dedicated themselves to the cause of God and to helping make ready a people to meet the Lord at the end of this life. These excelled in their climb up the rough side of the mountain.

References

Adventist Heritage Magazine. Loma Linda, California: Department of History and Political Science, Loma Linda University.

Adventist Review. Silver Spring, Maryland: Review and Herald Publishing Association, Sept. 1, 1904.

Andrews University Library Archives. Berrien Springs, Michigan: 1994.

Andross, Matilda Erickson. *Story of the Advent Message*. South Bend, Indiana: Review and Herald Publishing Association, 1926.

Baker, Delbert W. *The Unknown Prophet*. Hagerstown, Maryland: Review and Herald Publishing Association, 1987.

BaKhufu, Dr. Auset. *The Six Black Presidents—Black Blood: White Masks*. Washington, D. C.: PIKE Publications, 1993.

Bennett, Lerone, Jr. *Before the Mayflower—A History of Black America*. Chicago: Johnson Publishing Co., Inc., 1969.

Clark, Jerome L. *1844: Religious Movements, Vol. 1*. Brushton, New York: TEACH Services, Inc., 1996.

Davis, Cyrian. *The History of Black Catholics in the United States*. New York: The Crossroad Publishing Company, 1990.

Ellen G. White Estates. *In the Footsteps of the Pioneers*. Silver Spring, Maryland: E. G. White Estates, 1990.

Ellen G. White Estates. *Manuscript 56—1904*. Silver Spring, Maryland: General Conference of Seventh-day Adventists, 1990.

Encyclopedia Britannica 1968—William Bonton, Publisher—Chicago, London, Toronto, Geneva, Sydney, Tokyo, Manila.

Graybill, Ronald G. *E. G. White and Church Race Relations*. Washington, D. C.: Review and Herald Publishing Association, 1970.

Haley, Alex. *Roots*. Garden City, New York: Doubleday & Co., Inc., 1976.

Harding, Vincent. *There is a River*. New York: Harcourt Brace Jovanovich Publishers, 1981.

Hurt, James E., Jr. *National Assembly of Black Church Organizations*. New Orleans: First Assembly of Black Churches, 1984.

Hutchins, Fred L. *What Happened in Memphis*. Kingsport, Tennessee: Kingsport Press, Inc.

Jones, Ralph H. *Charles Albert Tindley—Prince of Preachers*. Nashville, Tennessee: Abingdon Press, 1982.

Justiss, Jacob. *Angels in Ebony*. Holland, Michigan: Jet Printing Service Company, 1975.

Kelly, J. N. D. *The Oxford Dictionary of Popes*.

King, Martin Luther. *Why We Can't Wait*. The New American Library, Inc., 1964.

Knight, Anna. *Mississippi Girl*. Nashville, Tennessee: Southern Publishing Association, 1952.

Knight, George R. *From 1888 to Apostasy*. Hagerstown, Maryland: Review and Herald Publishing Association, 1987.

Lakey, Othal Hawthorne. *The History of the CME Church*. Memphis, Tennessee: CME Publishing House, 1985.

Lincoln, C. Eric. *The Negro Pilgrimage in America*. Bantam Books, Inc., 1967.

Loughborough, J. N. *Rise and Progress of the Seventh-day Adventists*. Battle Creek, Michigan: General Conference of Seventh-day Adventists, 1891.

Loma Linda University, Department of Health and Political Science, *Adventist Heritage—A Journal of Adventist History*. Loma Linda, California, 1985.

McPherson, James M. *The Negro's Civil War*. New York: Ballantine Books, 1991.

The Ministerial Association. *Seventh-day Adventist Believe…27 Fundamental Doctrines*. Washington, D.C.: General Conference of Seventh-day Adventists, 1988.

National Geographic, Vol. 173, No. 1. Washington, D.C.: National Geographic Society, 1988.

National Geographic, Vol. 187, No. 5. Washington, D.C.: National Geographic Society.

Nichols, Francis D. *Ellen G. White and Her Critics*. Washington, D.C.: Review and Herald Publishing Association.

Oakwood College Archives. Huntsville, Alabama.

Ochs, Daniel A. and Grace Lillian. *The Past and Present Presidents— Biographies of the General Conference Presidents*. Nashville, Tennessee: Southern Publishing Association, 1974.

Olsen, A. V. *1888–1901—13 Crises Years*. Washington, D.C.: Review and Herald Publishing Association, 1981.

Powell, Ruth Marie. *Ventures in Education with Black Baptists in Tennessee*. New York: Carlton Press, Inc., 1979.

Reynolds, Louis B. *We Have Tomorrow*. Hagerstown, Maryland: Review and Herald Publishing Association, 1981.

Rogers, J. A. *The Five Negro Presidents—According to What White People Said They Were.* St. Petersburg, Florida: Helgam M. Rogers, 1965.

Russell, Sharman Apt. *Frederick Douglass.* Danbury, Connecticut: Grolier Inc., 1988.

The Seventh-day Adventist *Adult Sabbath School Lessons—Teacher's Edition.* Nampo, Idaho: Pacific Press Publishing Association, Oct., Nov., Dec.—1995.

Seventh-day Adventist Church Hymnal. Hagerstown, Maryland: Review and Herald Publishing Association, 1985.

Seventh-day Adventist Encyclopedia. Washington, D.C.: Review and Herald Publishing Association, 1976.

Songs of Zion Hymn Book. Nashville, Tennessee: Abingdon Press, 1981.

Styron, William. *The Confessions of Nat Turner.* New York: Random House, 1966.

Taylor, M. W. *Harriet Tubman.* New York: Chelsea House Publishers, 1991.

Thomsen, Russell J. *Seventh-day Baptists.* Mountain View, California: Pacific Press Publishing Association, 1971.

Tan, Thomas Twu-wee. *Your Chinese Roots.* Singapore: Times Books International, 1953.

Time Magazine, New York: Time Warner, Inc. , 1995.

Washington, Booker T. *Up from Slavery.* New York. Doubleday and Co., Inc., 1949.

Weslager, C. A. *Delaware's Forgotten Folk.* Philadelphia: University of Pennsylvania Press, 1943.

White, Arthur L. *The Elmshaven Years 1900–1905.* Washington, D.C.: Review and Herald Publishing Association, 1983.

White, Ellen G. *Counsels on Diets and Foods.* Mountain View, California: Pacific Press Publishing Association, 1948.

White, Ellen G. *Counsels on Health.* Mountain View, California: Pacific Press Publishing Association, 1951.

White, Ellen G. *The Desire of Ages.* Mountain View, California: Pacific Press Publishing Association, 1950.

White, Ellen G. *Early Writings.* Washington, D.C.: Review and Herald Publishing Association, 1942.

White, Ellen G. *Education.* Mountain View, California: Pacific Press Publishing Association, 1903.

White, Ellen G. *Evangelism.* Washington, D.C.: Review and Herald Publishing Association, 1946.

White, Ellen G. *The Great Controversy Between Christ and Satan.* Mountain View, California: Pacific Press Publishing Association, 1950.

White, Ellen G. *Life Sketches.* Mountain View, California: Pacific Press Publishing Association, 1915.

White, Ellen G. *Patriarchs and Prophets.* Mountain View, California: Pacific Press Publishing Association, 1948.

White, Ellen G. *Selected Messages.* Washington, D.C.: Review and Herald Publishing Association, 1958.

White, Ellen G. *The Southern Work.* Washington, D.C.: Review and Herald Publishing Association, 1966.

White, Ellen G. *Testimonies for the Church.* Mountain View, California: Pacific Press Publishing Association, 1948.

Index

Eunice 66
Evans, I. H. 145
Ewing, Brutus Howard 181
Finley, Elzira 122, 142
Fisk Jubilee Singers 17
Ford, Harry 12
Fords 182
Foss, Hazen 51, 58, 76
Foster, Stephen 139
Fountains 61, 181
Fox, Katherine 73
Fox, Margaret 73
Foye, William 12, 51, 56 - 58, 66, 75 - 76, 84
Foye, William E. 128
Frank, E. E. 111
Frazier, Albert 142
Frazier, Grace 141
Fraziers 61, 181
Frederick 111
Freeman, William O. 142, 170
Garnett, Henry Highland 21, 51, 53, 79, 88
Garrison, William Lloyd 53
Giddings, Philip 192
Gordon, M. D. 174
Gould, John 66
Graham, George 184
Grant, U. S. 147, 175
Grant, Ulysses S. 153
Graves 110
Graves, Ned 192
Gray, Charles A. 152
Gray, Ella 150, 152, 178
Gray, Emma 152
Gray, Harry 152, 178
Gray, Issac 152
Gray, Pearl 152
Gray, Rose 152
Graybill, Ron 179
Green, H. D. 134
Green, John 190
Green, W. H. 12, 194
Gregory, Pope 73, 98
Grimes, Etta 184
Grose, Ludwick 68
Guy, Grace 192

Hale, Frank W., Jr. 12, 104, 156
Haley, Alex 57, 140
Hall, Irwin 184
Hamilton 110
Hamilton, Alexander 50
Hamlin, Hannibal 50, 66
Hancock, Robert 184
Handy, William Christopher 147
Hansen, Louis A. 180
Harbor 141
Harding, Vincent 21
Harding, Warren G. 50, 192
Harmon, Elizabeth 63, 66
Harmon, Ellen 76
Harmon, Ellen Gould 63, 66, 76, 139
Harmon, Eunice 58
Harmon, Isaac 66
Harmon, John 66
Harmon, Robert 66
Harmons 50, 66
Haskel, Stephen N. 159
Hatcher, Doc C. 142
Hayden, Melvin 133 - 134
Hayes, Rutherford B. 153
Henri, C. 190
Henry, Archibald R. 154
Henson, Matthew 12
Herbert, Joseph 132
Hill 63
Hill, F. S. 144
Hill, Franklin Sydney 170
Hill, Zema 170
Hills 50
Himes, Joshua V. 78, 84
Hitler, Adolph 91, 191
Hodnet, Shirley 122
Holders 170
Holt, Mary 192
Hooks, Benjamin E. 28
Hottel 142
Howard, Oliver Otis 101, 194
Howard, T. M. R. S. 12, 121
Howe, Julia Ward 90, 139
Howell, R. B. C. 95
Hudsons 170
Humble, Alice 151
Humphrey, J. K. 134, 165
Humphreys 182

205